Walking:
the Changes

Walking: the Changes

Poetry by Linda M. Hasselstrom
Photographs by James W. Parker

Lame Johnny Press
PO Box 169
Hermosa, SD 57744

Walking: the Changes
© copyright 2022 Linda M. Hasselstrom and James W. Parker

Linda M. Hasselstrom is the author of:

Write Now, Here's How
Gathering from the Grassland: A Plains Journal
The Wheel of the Year: A Writer's Workbook
No Place Like Home: Notes From a Western Life
Between Grass and Sky: Where I Live and Work
Feels Like Far: A Rancher's Life on the Great Plains
Windbreak: A Woman Rancher on the Northern Plains
Going Over East: Reflections of a Woman Rancher
Land Circle: Writings Collected From the Land
Bison: Monarch of the Plains, and
The Roadside History of South Dakota, nonfiction
Poems collected in *Dakota: Bones, Grass, Sky*
Dirt Songs: A Plains Duet with Twyla M. Hansen
Dakota Bones, Bitter Creek Junction,
Roadkill, Caught By One Wing, When a Poet Dies

Co-Editor, *Leaning into the Wind, Woven on the Wind, Crazy Woman Creek*
Editor: *Journal of a Mountain Man*

James W. Parker has written the following:

A Disappearing Agrarian Landscape
Stories Told In Things Left Behind
Southwestern Sojourn: A Photographer's Journal
What I Learned Climbing the Grand Teton

Published by Lame Johnny Press, Linda M. Hasselstrom, editor
PO Box 169, Hermosa, S.D. 57744-0169
lindamichele777@gmail.com

ISBN 978-0-917624-08-7

Dedication

This book is dedicated to Jerry Ellerman, who upon his retirement from thirty years with the Wyoming Highway Department, came with me to this South Dakota ranch where I grew up. He thought moving here rather than to the northwest, where his family lives, a fair trade for my seventeen years of living with him in Cheyenne, Wyoming.

We created a harmonious new life here, as he built practical and beautiful furniture and other items in his workshop, and I built poems and stories in my study. We envisioned a serene future together. He enthusiastically joined with me in giving back to this community which has given so much to me. We both acknowledged that I, being ten years older than he, would die first, leaving him free to remain here, or join family members in another part of the country.

Many of these poems were written or completed in what turned out to be the last year of his life. I began planning to self-publish this collection soon after our arrival in South Dakota. I was looking forward to showing him the poems he'd influenced by his kindness, his patience, his generosity, his love.

He was killed on the highway only three miles from our home on September 18, 2020. My life here without him will never be complete.

Jerry L. Ellerman, December 27, 1952 to September 18, 2020

He was my North, my South, my East and West,
My working week and my Sunday rest,
My noon, my midnight, my talk, my song;
I thought that love would last forever; I was wrong.

The stars are not wanted now; put out every one,
Pack up the moon and dismantle the sun,
Pour away the ocean and sweep up the wood;
For nothing now can ever come to any good.

    — W. H. Auden, "Funeral Blues"

Foreword

When you meet Linda Hasselstrom or James Parker in person or through their art, you will have found what's best about South Dakota. There are stories everywhere in the prairies and hills. Linda's writing, her books, essays, and poems explore the landscape and tell stories of her life in words. James's photographs tell stories of the land, of forgotten places and lives, through light, shadow, and color.

When my sons were in high school, Ms. Hasselstrom was a teacher of writing. All three sons are now middle-aged fathers and published authors who remember her workshops. With one of their children currently writing a screenplay, her influence carries on. I have acquired a collection of Linda's books over the years, and with each one I say, this is the best. And each time I'm right. I believe I've gotten to know her through her writing. Her words paint pictures with remarkable clarity and honesty, as scenes of life as a writer and woman rancher on the South Dakota grassland come alive. Now that we've met, shared a bagel or two and become actual friends, I know the humanity and sincerity behind those written words.

James W. Parker is a dear personal friend as well as a friend of my family. He is also an author and my co-conspirator in the business of books. I first met his mother untold years ago. She and I have a catalog of late-night email exchanges through which we shared life stories, both of us strangers in a strange new land that welcomed two young easterners as brides and offered us a wholesome place to grow a bright little garden of children. James's mother introduced me to his father, Dr. Watson Parker, acclaimed professor of history, lecturer, and author of some of the most respected and enduring books of South Dakota history. With wit and wisdom, Dr. Parker was South Dakota's own Mark Twain. And so it went. Over the years I've gotten to know James and many of this family of historians, writers, teachers, lecturers, artists, tour guides, hikers, and lovers of all things South Dakota. Good people, every one.

Although I have suggested it at least twice, only Linda Hasselstrom knows how many times she has respectfully declined nominations to be South Dakota's Poet Laureate. She has accrued a long list of awards and achievements and is well deserving of her membership in the South Dakota Hall of Fame.

When you read a book or see a work of art you enter someone else's passion and imagination, but you can also find yourself there. *Walking: The Changes* is such a book. You can find your humanity in the misery of corporate-created pollution in *Eulogy for Bhopal*. "In Bhopal husbands divorce wives whose children died in their wombs." In *What If*, you might also wonder what it would be like had you chosen a different path, "If I lived here I'd walk to Decker's Market, chat about the weather while the girl rang up my groceries… watch the trains rumble past…" You will occasionally face decisions that affect other living beings, as in *The Spider in the Bathroom Window*, "I open the window, slide a spatula under her… smiling as I do this small service for a world where so many people shudder in the grip of despots." In the harshness of winter, summer will return with the juice of a plum in *Bottling August* as it "blooms in my mouth…" Love forgotten or lost will return in *My Wedding Ring* where removing it "will never erase you from my heart." And we can't help relating with frustration when autocorrect insists on correcting our words despite our hammering away at the keys, trying to say "place mat", and not "placenta."

It takes a poet to "watch the spruce trees bow, ladylike, their skirts a gentle shimmy," or to simply learn how to exit the world gracefully from a dying friend. Every photograph that accompanies these poems is a love song to a memory. James finds beauty in the past and we find stories without words. Who lived here and how did they get here? What did they do and why did they leave? They left parts of themselves behind as weather and time gradually erode what remains. That cartwheel says so much. His photographs appear in several of his own books while enlarged copies decorate the walls of some fortunate homeowners. Two poets, one with photographs, one with words, both children of western South Dakota who understand this landscape, have collaborated to produce a lovely book filled with compassion, humility, and gentle humor.

— ***Ann Haber Stanton, November 2022***

Preface

Some of these poems have been previously published, as noted in the acknowledgments. I revised some poems after their first publication, before including them here.

Though I have a thorough grounding in the standard forms of poetry (an M.A. in American Literature from the University of Missouri), I love to experiment. I also believe that it's too easy for a formally-trained poet with a couple of literature degrees to fall into the habit of writing in strict formats and assuming only those methods matter to all poets.

So, to recapture my enjoyment of poetry after decades of writing, reading, and commenting on it for other writers at Windbreak House Retreats, I sometimes play. For example, in writing *Coronavirus Spring*, I challenged myself to write a daily observation in ten syllables per line, with forty syllables to a stanza.

I am never far from a notebook. I started *Lockdown* on the yellow pad on the table beside the cast iron tub where I frequently treat my aches and pains with a hot bath scented with odors intended to calm the mind and soothe the skin. In that bath, I was reflecting on how happy our lives were, under conditions many people might have considered limited. We separated each morning, me to my office and Jerry to his workshop, and both worked happily on our own projects all day except for lunch and dinner.

Jerry bought the tub for me when the houses of well-deserved "ill repute" in Deadwood were selling their contents after being closed down. In my bedroom that night was a rose plant he'd given me for Valentine's Day, knowing I disliked bouquets that wilted in a few days. I planned to plant it in our sheltered garden where he'd built raised beds and filled them with rich earth for the Early Girl tomatoes we loved.

Two weeks later, Jerry was dead. The rose died not long afterward. I'm glad I wrote the poem when I did.

The lesson: don't wait for inspiration. Write it now, no matter how hurried you are, no matter how rough the resulting draft. Scribble on napkins, on menus, on tickets from the grocery store. Always carry a notebook or something to write on.

The honor of being named South Dakota's first Living Poet of Merit in 2020 astonished me, because this state is full of poets, as well as of people who have not yet begun to write. (I'm not going to say the honor "humbles" me; that's a pitiful cliché and of course I'm proud to represent my home state in this way!) I hope my work presents a vivid contrast with some of the other people who profess to represent our state in public. Part of the job of a living poet of any merit at all, I believe, is to encourage people to express—especially to write—their ideas, thoughts, observations, no matter what form they choose. I hope this book is an inspiration to all of you.

I regard everything in my life as possible material for writing. When I'm washing dishes, I may be thinking of the way my grandmother's sterling silver shines through the suds, or how much I love the deep blue color of the plates. My pockets and purse always contain tiny notebooks so I can capture thoughts that might escape. No matter what unrelated chores I have done all morning, by noon I have a handful of ideas that might turn into finished poetry or prose. Or remain as scribbled notes into eternity.

So my advice to all who would be poets or serious writers in any genre, or family record keepers, or newspaper reporters, or diarists, is always to have a means of recording your thoughts. I'm told that personal phones can accomplish this task these days, but that's just a rumor to me since I have an ancient flip phone. Whatever method you choose to record your thoughts, hang onto them: they might become poems, prose, or letters to your aged aunt. All have value; write them down as soon as they arrive.

Poetry is everywhere in the world; make it your pleasure—if not your job—to record it.

— *Linda M. Hasselstrom, October 2022*

Table of Contents

The End of a Beginning   **81**

Acknowledgments & Notes on Poems   **106**

Introduction to the Photographs   **109**

Notes on Photographs   **110**

Meet the Authors   **114**

Poems for George R. Snell

These poems celebrate a man, George R. Snell, Linda Hasselstrom's husband from 1978 until his death September 7, 1988 from the effects of chemotherapy for Hodgkins' disease. They were published by Potter Press in an edition of 150 copies in 1994-1995, for George's friends, as a celebration of their respect and love for him.

White Buffalo
— *For Gina and the Spirit Canoe*

In the hospital, nurses pad
on rubber-soled feet.
Doors are closed. My husband's
Oxygen bubbles in the corner.
"This is a terrible way to die," he says,
"slowly suffocating."

A white buffalo stands
at the hall's end. His mane
brushes the ceiling; frost
glitters on his beard. He stomps
a black hoof, shakes his head.
Ice shards clatter
on marble but no one hears.
His horns punch the ceiling.

His breath chills, blows papers.
He walks; the building rumbles.
"B-1 taking off," says an airman,

blind to buffalo. There are no lights
on the landing field. The buffalo
passes the nurses' station,
picking up speed; gallops
into this room.

George opens deep blue eyes.
The buffalo bellows once,
leaps to the bed;
both of them are gone.

Outside, the shape
of a tall man is drawn
against the stars. He strides
as if he knows where he's going,
glances back over his shoulder.
He winks at me, smiles,
goes.

Linda M. Hasselstrom & James W. Parker

George's Poem

Required few words.
Even dying, he kept it simple:
"Be happy. Watch the sunsets."

What kind of philosophy is that
To get me through the next forty years?
I have to figure it out by myself—
but that's not new.
He believed I could.

He helped me up if I fell,
but he didn't grab my arm
when I strode ahead.
When I cried and clung to him
On his hospital bed,
he muttered, "Don't get too poetic."
George's poem is one doe

Standing knee-deep in Slate Creek.
She scratches an ear
with a shiny-wet hoof.
A man and a woman read in sunlight

on a lichen-covered rock
rearing out of autumn snow.
Near a blue tent,
a white dog chases gophers.

Walking at dusk, they hear a fawn
wail in fear and cold.
All night the dog sleeps between them.
At dawn, snow collapses the tent.
Entangled, they all crawl out
Laughing, throw snowballs, make
coffee. The fawn's tracks cross
the meadow beside his mother's.

Now he is dead, I remember
how he smiled as he drank coffee.
He was writing a poem with no words.
I cannot read it in a book.

No one else
will ever read it at all.

Digging the Bulbs

Dear Wilford,
This afternoon I dug gladioli bulbs.
Autumn sun warmed my back; I lifted
each bulb carefully, whacked off
the stalks with the knife he kept sharp
for me. With naked hands
I sifted dark earth for the baby bulbs.
You taught me to save them each year,
watch them send up tiny leaves
until they were large enough to bloom.
Your hands popped new white bulbs
from shriveled brown husks.

Each year I would think of you and Beth,
laboring together on that dry farm
to produce new plants, save those that might disappear.
When you wrote me last, she was dead.
You sent a photograph of the gladiolus named for her.
You didn't want to live.

My husband planted railroad ties in the earth
as a border for my flowers.
He died a month ago.

I am digging these bulbs for the last time.
Lately I have done many things for the last time.
I'll give these bulbs to a friend.

Each spring I've remembered
the way you smiled at each other,
wrinkles disappearing into love;
each summer when I cut blooms
I saw your faces turned to each other.
When you wrote to tell me she had died,
I did not know what to say,
I cried, did nothing.

Now I know to tell you only
that I care, that I remember.
We have worked in partnership
with the friendly earth for years.
Now both our loves lie in the cold dark.
What am I to make of this?
I use the spading fork to lift another clump,
reach deep to raise the knobby bulbs
into the light.

Windbreak Now

My book about our life together filled
two hundred thirty-three closely-spaced pages.
The title was what everyone needs on the plains,
and what you meant to me:
a windbreak against the cold,
between my trips into politics,
workshops, blizzards of loneliness.
You died—not slowly like our trees
for lack of water—
too fast for me to follow.
My life has changed in every way.
I don't save scraps of meat to make soup stock;
canning jars boxed in the garage hold dust;
my complexion brush scrubs mushrooms;
the apples in the freezer won't make pies.

I stand on the deck in starlit dark
and talk to you, feel you close—
but ghosts don't break real wind.
You still stand between me
and a world I love but don't like much.
I see that look when I think revenge
or say things mean and small.
You're inside me like a second heart,
beating a little out of time with mine.
I feel your breathing
against my chest in the good nights,
slower, longer breaths going deeper.
Outside, at seventy below zero,
I wear your coats and overalls—
my windbreak now.

The Glacier on Crystal Lake
--The stomach of a mammoth found entombed in ice contained yellow buttercups from its last meal.

I've sat in a leaky boat over the blue line
for six months, anchored,
staring at the glacial face
of your life. It's all there: layers of dust,
years of deep snowfall, pictures from
your childhood, frozen.

Last night your grandfather died.
The glacier calved; a chunk of ice
the size of a house rocked
my fragile shell, floats
beside me now, melting,
spinning in cold blue water.
Pieces of your life
are growing smaller as I watch.

Soon I will unship the oars,
row back to the village. Tonight
by trembling oil lamps
smaller than my cupped hand,
I will tell your stories—

how your grandfather took
you fishing, eating cinnamon rolls
and drinking RC Cola, built an ice boat
to sail Crystal Lake, ran from
the bees through the orchard, down
the hill, up to the barn loft,
into the lake.

Later, when the oil burns low,
I'll tell alone
the stories we told together,
yours and mine.
After the lamps go out,
in the warm, rustling dark
I will whisper new stories
that will be mine alone.

Far in the ocean,
the color of your eyes,
the glacier will crash and rumble
into the deep.

Valentine's Night

You didn't like Valentine's Day,
going to the mall to find a card
among fake flowers.
Surprised, I dried the roses
you brought last year,
saved the pink heart box.
I keep your letters in it;
your grave is six months old.
My mother sent a card.

Moonlight lurks behind clouds;
I stand under a silver ceiling.
Snow falls; coyotes sing of romance.
Wearing your socks,
I shuffle a heart huge on the deck,
scribble promises in frost on the rail.

Cheyenne River Valley at Wasta

Four mares guard four colts,
lying so sprawled they might be dead.
The car swoops at seventy down dry slate hills
pinned together with cedar.

Folded into a hill is a green gully,
edged with plum bushes about to bloom,
cedar for shelter, a thin blade of water.
I know your lodge is there, hidden.
you camped here for the silence of spring,
to read, fish, watch the hills green up.

Everywhere, I see places you might be.
At first I searched them all.
But now I know if you are there,
I'll find no proof.
Sometimes I wave,
or shout my love
on the wind of my speed.

Your body is making grass on a clay hill,
but you are in every pleasant valley;
You stand by each trout stream,
making the line sing over the water.

I have never known these hidden spots
So well as now,
through the eyes of a red-tail hawk
that drops out of the wind
then spins away to some other sky.

Drought Year

I dreamed I slept alone in a drought year,
and now I do.
I lie in the short grass;
water is a dream.
All day I was fuel for the sun
burning like wildfire over a dry land.
Ghosts of streams slash earth,
water's memory
ripples in sandstone.

I dreamed you died in a drought year,
And you did. Now
I dream water all night long:
hear it laughing in the throat of a cloud,
imagine dry grass brushing the house
is rain. When the killdeer cries
At the edge of the dry pond,
I add my plea to hers
in a voice husky with dust.

I dreamed myself a dry woman,
and I am, the juice gone
out of me. My skin is fragrant
with prairie odors.
I am drying grass, wind-bent.

Long tough roots grapple
seep into baked prairie earth.
leaves die, but roots dream
in crumbled sod,
wait for rain.

Wolves

I know your pirate face,
your eagle nose, scarred throat,
at any time of day,
any mood or season.
I know all of you
in the dark, your cough
your mountain scent
in a sweating crowd.
Every inch of me
would know any inch of you.

Now I know your swollen grave
by smoking red sunset,
by ice-white moonlight,
by snow drifted into deer tracks
between the rocks.
I've seen an eagle spiral up
at sunset over your mound.

In the wolf hour
I've heard you howling on my scent,
tasted your touch,
seen your wolf soul.
You find me constant,
staring into the dark.

Thanksgiving Prayer

Behind me, the black shadow of a church
Reaches out from every height in Scotland.
Through chaotic centuries, their stone hymns
drown screams, the whine of sword blades.
Conflicting legends paint their floors
with the thick, red blood of martyrs;
smoke from human flesh sketches
separate creeds against blue sky.
From their aisles blows a chill Christian wind
driving men and women to their knees
in the blood of their own ancestors,
their own children.

Surrounded by ancient churches—
with the opulent liquor of entreaty, hymns
and Christian sanctity oozing from their stones—
I pray on the beach.
Empty my pockets of stones
and shells from stormy coasts,
place them in a circle around sage from home.
Earth lies quiet under my feet; air sweeps past
in storm clouds; rain runs down my face;
warmth from my heart and fingers
stands for the fourth element, fire.

The salt stings my throat, scorched raw
by years of bawling adoration
into empty stone vaults and naves,
of begging stone-eared saints
to turn their sleepy smiles on me.
My eyes burn with tears
for love I'll never know again.
Sharp-tongued Cuillin Hills chant ferocious love
from heather heights to lakes filled with tears.
Today he walked beside me.
inside his coat, I crawled down the tunnel
to the burial crypt.
I did not lie down.

Now I stand facing sea wind.
White foam sweeps away the lighter stones,
the sagebrush and tobacco.
I ask only to come back here;
salt spray eases the pain in my throat.
The hand inside my pocket clutches heather
dug between the standing stones.
When I get home, I will plant it
on my husband's grave.

Late March Blizzard

Ankle deep in mud that wants
to suck us down before our time,
we plod through the corral, pitch
hay, fight to get birthing cows
into the barn, drag dead calves
outside. Snow falls so thick
it's hard to recognize familiar cows,
each other's blurred faces.
We are tired and cranky, mud and blood
up to our knees. Our minds squeeze down to
a fire, coffee, dry clothes.

                    A cry
raises our eyes. Two blue herons
circle. Like a Chinese painting.
Their angled breasts prow
against the snow, lifting with each beat
of the mighty wings.

We sail into the falling snow,
twin graceful shapes who know mud—and more.
Our fragile feet are not stuck in clay;
we pose in a cottonwood,
then lift,
        disappear into time.

***Land Circle: Writings Collected From the Land,
Fulcrum, 1991***

Old Friends

They came until the halls bulged, the air trembled
With balloons and flowers. Children's drawings clung
to the walls, photographs crowded the table.
The tall man in black, his famous scythe
disguised as a briefcase, had to elbow
through, even with an appointment.
No one tried to stop him,
but no one got out of his way, either.

George made him sit at the end of the bed, listen.
We all told stories: whoever sat beside George
held his right hand; he could still feel that.
Death kept clearing his throat,
pointing to his watch, fingering the catch
on his briefcase. Everyone ignored him.

Finally, he caught on, told a joke,
Told stories about George, how they'd met before.
He admitted admiration for the man's direct
blue gaze, the way George threw him out.
This time he knew he'd win, but he played

by the rules: none of that grim faceless stuff,
No swinging the wailing scythe, no tears.
He threw back his hood, laughed for
the first time in years.

Campfires flared in the bright room, drinks
were shared, domes shingled, parties planned,
enjoyed, over. Tipis were pitched, struck,
folded; fish were caught; deer were shot at,
missed.

Among the folks at the cemetery, in clothes
as wildly varied as their natures,
Death's outfit didn't turn a head.
He kept his distance from the mountain men
and honor guard.

                    Someone said
he and George walked off
toward the smoky sunset mountains,
fishing poles over their shoulders.

Things Worth Doing

Predator

That teardrop
shape is a hawk
upright on the white
branch of the dead cottonwood.
Frost cloaks the hillside.
Fog shrouds the sky.
Black hawk head
slowly turns,
eyes seek.
Mouse.
Blood.
Red.

Reading the Newspaper in the Back Yard

Two Marines die in mortar fire in Baghdad.
Four red tulips open in front of the house.
Searchers find the child dead; a green
plaster cast still cradles her broken arm.
Iris spears rise sharp above last year's
dry curls. An earthquake shakes L.A.
Clematis shoots from sawdust
to climb the arbor's trellised wall.
A soldier dies in "a non-hostile incident."
Daffodils open beside the old cottonwood.
In Veracruz a gas leak kills six people.
Buds swell the twisted branches of a lilac.
A rebel bomb explodes in a crowd.
A Texas county's first female sheriff
is also Hispanic, a lesbian, and a Democrat.

Blue bells bloom
on the same day
as last year.

The Traveling Poet is Going Home

Toothbrush, toothpaste,
shampoo, rinse. As I use
each one, it leaves
the spotlight on the bathroom shelf,
slips into the black bag.
Soap, lipstick. Lotion.
Finally the glass stage is empty,
nothing reflected but
that wrinkle between my eyebrows.

The mirror waits
for the woman who will spritz
my face away, leave the reflection
clean and empty,
waiting for the next face to check in.

When I close the door behind me,
the pillows fluff themselves.
The room inhales.

The woman who cleans the mirror
never looks into it. She wipes
two dozen mirrors in a day,
reflects
            in none of them.

Which Face is Real, Which Remembered?

I don't remember your real face
above me as I lay in our bed,
only a series of publicity shots
in which your lying mouth is frozen
in that seductive smile that worked
so well on so many women. I never look
at your Facebook page.

Instead, I summon up
A kind face: Mrs. Elsie Enders. I can see
both her chins, the way her belly shook
when she laughed. When my mother
married that rancher and we moved
to the country, Mrs. Enders led
the new girl into that classroom where
all the other kids had known each other
since birth. I don't remember what she said,
but her arm around me was enough
to make me smile
                    at her tombstone today.

Sometimes, still, your face intrudes
if I think of the past. You have a way
of taking over a woman's mind.
When you show up today, I am walking a beach
beside a tangled swamp where hands
reach up, limbs thrash in muck.
Faint cries echo off the trees,
twist and welter in the vines.
Somewhere a sun shines but light
does not penetrate that murky past.

I turn away, leave those scenes behind--
again—take one step and then another.
Watch how my bare feet claim the sand,
how the ocean takes it back. Fog
rolls in behind me, but ahead
I see a grassy plain
alive with birds that sing.

What to Do at Teton Science School
— for all the students

Look at the *"Scat of the Day"*;
guess which animal deposited it.
Estimate velocity of ejection. Giggle.
Feel the mounted pronghorn's face.
Giggle. Braid the stuffed mountain
sheep's beard. Giggle. Stare at the talons
of the great horned owl. Giggle.
Find your skis and mittens, go outside.
Take pictures of the Tetons. Giggle.

Hold your nose at the mothball smell
as you study the cotton eye of a raven
Olas Murie stuffed in 1934. Kneel before
a rough-legged hawk. Do not giggle.
Look into the photographed eyes
of Mardy Murie in her wagon
fifty years ago. Cut firewood.
Take pictures of the Tetons.

Wonder what she was thinking,
when she agreed to honeymoon in Alaska
with a man who stuffed ravens
and made her cut firewood.
Ski Ditch Creek, watch the jaws
of a moose eating willow. Kneel
inside a quinzhe. Breathe. Look
for your mittens. Quietly. Do not giggle.
Snap on skis. Practice lifting your heels.
Take pictures of the Tetons.

Pick yourself up. Untangle your skis.
Watch snow curl, sag, slide down roofs.
Set mouse traps. Count aspen shadows.
Watch a red squirrel eat gorp.
Find your mittens on someone else's skis
stuck in a snowbank behind the cabin.
Go home. Throw away
your pictures of the Tetons.

Wicca

Gray forms leap
over flames that snatch.
Red sparks flick,
vanish against obsidian sky.
Tonight we touch
pirouette, remember,
and give thanks.
Sage and sweetgrass smoke
drifts among pines
grown thicker than blood.
A single talon,
a patch of scaly hide,
break the water's sheen
in the scrying bowl.
Some of us will be
warm flesh tomorrow.
Some of us
will still be cold.

Eulogy for Bhopal

Q: What do you get when you cross two nation states, a large corporation, forty tons of poison, and at least eight thousand dead human beings?

A. Retirement with full pay and benefits (Warren Anderson, CEO of Union Carbide)

--*The Age of Ooops*, Derrick Jensen, Orion, March April 2011

The chairman of the board has a kindly face. He breathes deeply
before he speaks. Victims of the gas gasp for breath, vomit.
The chairman of the board is appalled. Women suffered abortions
as they ran from the gas. The chairman of the board says
employees stop him in the hall to express their sorrow at the accident.
In Bhopal, husbands divorce wives whose children died in their wombs.
The chairman is calm. The women bleed irregularly. The chairman
of the board responds patiently to questions. Victims run high fevers.
The chairman shakes his head solemnly. Women walk the streets
sobbing with hunger. The chairman of the board says Union Carbide
offers two hundred thirty million dollars in settlement for all the claims
of the living. All the claims. Of the living. Almost four thousand
die immediately. Smoke from the cremation of people and animals
chokes the living. Two hundred thirty million dollars, he repeats with respect.
The reporters nod and mutter. That's a lot of money. The women smell
of rotting flesh. Indian government officials say lawsuits may
 total one hundred billion dollars. Victims' eyes burn and blur.
All this legal action will take time, says the chairman of the board.
No relief programs are geared specifically to the problems
of women. Indian government officials say they want
five billion dollars. The chairman of the board says
he's answered enough questions. At home, his wife
makes a dry martini, just the way he likes it. She showers,
slides into bed freshly scented, with no smelly discharge.
A week later, a West Virginia plant releases the same gas.
No one dies. The story vanishes from front pages.

Surveys done by the Bhopal campaign groups have shown this toxic waste, which according to their tests contains six of the persistent organic pollutants banned by the UN for their highly poisonous impacts on the environment and human health, has now reached 42 areas in Bhopal and continues to spread. Dec 8, 2019

Linda M. Hasselstrom & James W. Parker

Letter to Anne
— *for Anne Laura Meiners, 1911-2008*

The book was dusty, tucked into a shelf
with old school texts but when I opened it,
I recognized your hand:
              Fifty years ago
you wrote their names—Thomas, Christine, John,
Robert, Milton. Three in second grade;
none in third; two in fourth and fifth;
five in sixth grade, three in seventh,
two in eighth.
                  The second-graders were then
eight years old, the oldest students thirteen.
Eighteen of them in that one room.
                       Not only
did you keep them orderly, you taught
them well. Thomas tells me every single
one of them went to college.
If they squabbled during recess,
You'd purse your lips and quietly suggest
they leave their arguments outside. They'd pledge
allegiance, then you'd set them all to work.
You'd talk with every one, from tots to teens,
respecting how each young brain worked.

All this
I've only heard. You never were my teacher,
and now I'm sorry for that fact. You were
my aunt, my father's sister, the woman
named to raise me if my parents died.
You loved me, I suppose, but you were never
blinded to my faults. At family dinners
you might ask me what my college courses were,
judge my answers for yourself, and tell
my parents what you thought. You told me,
how important schooling was.
                       At dinner
all the talk was politics, important
issues. When you disagreed with father
you were polite but firm. He told my mother
what to think, but never you. When he
got sarcastic, you resisted anger.
I listened and I learned.
                   Your little school
was moved and turned into a storage shed.
When I pass it, I think of you.
You were not my teacher, but you are.

Wearing Your Socks to Bed
— *for George Randolph Snell, 1942-1988*

Your socks are size twelve. Every night I pull a pair
over my size eight-and-a-half—OK, OK, size nine—feet.
The toes flop over unless I yank them up over my calves.
Then I can slide between the cold sheets,
breathe deep and sleep, my head still turned
toward the side where you always slept.
I'm still sleeping in our marriage bed,
but another man and two new dogs sleep beside me.

You bought wool socks every chance you got,
on sale in fancy stores, or from Army Surplus.
You kept them in your duffel, filled drawers,
tucked them in our sleeping bags. Even stuffed
them into niches in the old blue van.
"You never know," you said, "when you're gonna
need extra socks. If we got stalled in a blizzard
we could pick up other people like Jack Lintz did that time.
They'd all be warm, wearing socks on their feet and hands,
maybe even on their heads, as big as mine are."

When no one knew what to get you for birthdays
and Christmas, I'd say, "Wool socks!" And to my mother,
"Not those cheap thin cotton ones like you got last year.
All-Wool. Size 12." She'd shudder and complain about the cost,
buy one pair, wrap them with more handkerchiefs. After you died,
I counted all the handkerchiefs you hadn't even opened--
forty-two, as I recall—gave them to Good Will.

I sold your van. But I kept the socks. I tucked a pair
into my toolbox, a pair in every suitcase, sleeping bag
and trunk. I must have worn out twenty pair, but every year
I find a few more. Lately I wear them in the daytime too:
electric blue with denim skirts, pure deep red on lively days.
Long skirts hide the orange ones, but the black ones
go with everything. My feet are always cold.

Mother's been gone six or seven years, my dad fifteen.
This birthday I'll turn sixty-four, while you are always
forty-two. I remember how I put my icy feet against your back
each night. Colder every year, my feet keep walking
toward the cold you've felt for all these years.

From the Dinosaur Factory
— *for George Randolph Snell and Bill Schulz*

Connie is "getting through" her divorce
by pretending she's married—
to Sylvia Plath. She tells me
about her student Danny
who is getting through high school
by growing and mowing
the hair on her legs
into a Mohawk.

Kathy adopted more cats,
moved again,
got married again,
changed her name again.

Wendy, driving the dusty road
between Red Scaffold and Spearfish,
looks for falling stars. She hacked off
her long blonde hair, but smiles
with her eyes wet and jokes about
her sisters-in-law, the White Wolf women
who hate her.

Bill reads poetry
in a dinosaur factory
loud with three redhaired sons,
none old enough for school yet,
who can all pronounce tyrannosaur.

Bette eats out three times a day,
never lets anyone see her cry,
goes to meetings of both her daughters'
lesbian support groups.

I drink too much,
talk to Bette's son, my husband
who has been dead three months.
I write poems to remember how
we all get through this,
hoping to
figure out why.

My Wedding Ring

— for George Randolph Snell

Twice before I've slipped it off. We were no longer
quite married—wed, espoused, united, joined
--when your funeral was over. A year later,
I met a man who promised much. He wasn't evil,
but he was looking for someone else,
possibly himself. I put the ring back on.

On the second anniversary of your death,
I removed the ring again, read the inscription,
"In Beauty May I Walk." Then
I put it back on, to walk
highland moors with our best friend.

Tonight, this third solstice after your death,
I took it off amid a circle of chanting friends,
between drumbeats that made the red moon throb
in the east. A circle of gold.
Wearing it didn't make me true to you.
Removing it will never
erase you from my heart.

I met George Randolph Snell when I was teaching for
a year at Black Hills State College (now University)
in Spearfish, S.D. In a tiny street near my house, I
was walking the black Scottie my first husband had
abandoned when he ran off after his latest girlfriend. I'd
noticed the little green house at the end of the street,
but never seen anyone near it. George and a friend
were sitting on the porch, drinking beer. I heard them
talking, the friend urging George to speak to me. I had
straightened my back and turned away, ready to rebuff
any advances in spite of the fact that he was tall, broad-
shouldered, handsome, with long brown hair.

George said, "Hey lady, where'd you get the funny-
looking dog?"

I laughed. I have no memory of what happened next,
but he became my beloved second husband. He died in
1988 from the effects of Hodgkins' disease.

Grass Speaks to Fences

I. Cheyenne, Wyoming
Inside my fence, cottonwood trees
chatter to ash and apple, stoic
currant bushes guard the borders.
Woodbine twines on fences,
lupine opens blue mouths
singing to snow-in-summer
pale as wind. Gossiping, the plants
pretend they do not live on this dry plain,
because I give them water.

Dusty yarrow froths pink, daylilies
announce themselves in orange headlines.
Feverfew washes away my headaches.
Balloon flowers and tarragon tremble
beside arugula. Johnny Jumps Up.
Rhubarb thrives beside hollyhocks, horseradish.
Outside the fence, sage waits
with penstemon for the city
to run out of water.

II. South Dakota
The only fences here are barbed wire
between us and the cows. Grass thrives:
redtop, fescue, grama, needlegrass, foxtail,
bluestem, buffalo grass, timothy. In the garden
bindweed creeps under pumpkin vines;
asparagus and rhubarb conspire.
Beans and peas cling to their trellis;
lettuce and radishes, carrots, turnips, all
crowd together, watching each others' backs.

Horizon to horizon, skyline to sky,
native grasses wait, whispering,
"Get over green. Renounce hoses.
Learn to live with plants that can
defend themselves. Learn to love
sharp edges."

Women Talking

Road-weary, I hardly notice the sign
outside the pizza joint:
"Free Beer to Winning Softball Teams."
Smells ripple like water through the crowded room—
sweat, dirt, blood, more sweat. I reel
into the last empty booth and order.
The room is filled with big men
sitting shoulder to tan shoulder.
And with big women, all talking.
The men's voices tumble and surge,
rattle the rafters. "Him and his father
and brother all farm together, you know.
He said they're four hundred thousand bucks
in debt. He told me, "Hell,
no way we're all gonna make it."

The women jiggle babies draped
over thick brown arms, roll their eyes,
pour beer. I see their lips moving,
dive deep into the river of noise
to hear the murmur:
"She's as proud
of that baby as if it had a daddy, ain't she?"
Eyes narrowed, they look at the girl, then
at the jostling men. "Wonder who he's gonna
look like most?" says the pregnant one.
"If he looks like my Charlie, I'll take a butcher knife
to him. Charlie, I mean."
                              Laughing, a skinny woman
in a t-shirt bawls, "Best way to keep him home,
honey. Cut too deep, though, he'll be like me!"

Under the snickers, a gray-haired woman asks,
"Say, does that youngest Bolton boy seem
a little slow to you?"
A redhead answers,
snapping her gum, "No slower than his daddy,

and look how rich he is!" A beefy blonde says,
"Yeah. His paw left him the place free and clear.
It's only taken him ten years to build up
the biggest debt in the state." An older woman
with rhinestone glasses nods.
"He'll probably run for office. Ain't that
about what it takes to be governor?"

The rapids of their laughter sweeps
my mind back to twenty-five years ago,
the last time I came to this town. High school,
some school group, probably debate.
The grownup who'd been stuck with us
for days must have thought we'd learn humility
if we toured the state hospital.
We'd lurched down slime-green halls,
goggling at rooms packed with beds
filled with people who were retarded,
maimed, insane. Our clever comments ebbed
to whispers. I stared longest at a man
with a trim black mustache. His gigantic head
wobbled on the pillow; his body was a baby's,
wearing nothing but a diaper. He glared
at me from eyes black as his hair. He was
thirty-five, they said. He might live
another fifty years, diapered in that bed.

Caught in the eddy of the restaurant booth,
I realize that's thirty years ago. He might still be there,
lying in the dark. I float the current
of the women's talk. They know his story,
might tell me if I asked. A younger brother
might be sitting with a team of winners.
I pay my bill, speed up as I pass the hospital.
"Goodbye," I say to the mustached man,
and to the women who will keep his story.

I'm Going to Have to Buy Another Ham

With thanks to Nancy Curtis

First it was breast cancer,
and they never quite controlled it.
She was a nurse, so she tried
everything: had a hysterectomy so
it wouldn't lurk there. Went to Johns
Hopkins for a clinical trial. Meanwhile,
she kept busy, working as the school nurse.
She started a Wellness Center; they've named it
after her. Started a program to help people
after surgery; visited cancer patients.
Worked with mine officials to prevent
accidents. After she got too sick,
she worked from home. Then
it got into her brain. They say
they've done all they can.
She's forty-nine.

A month ago I bought
a ham sliced thin because
she'd been given two weeks
to live. Since then, I've been
to three funerals. To every one,
I took thin slices of ham wrapped
around either cheese or asparagus,
and she's still alive. She quit eating
two weeks ago. She can't talk. Can't
see. When people come to visit,
she holds her eyelids open with
one hand while she scribbles
notes with the other,
teaching us
how to die.

The Spider in the Bathroom Window

couldn't get out.
Every time I noticed her,
she was poised near the top
of the screen, or flicking a strand
of her immaculate web to test
the tension. Two days ago, she caught
a mosquito that had followed
me inside, trapped when I shut
the window. I haven't seen her eat
today.

      Where's my spider book?
Basilica spider—that looks like her, but those
are found in Western meadows.

Bolas? No, the markings aren't right.
My favorite, Argiope, I hope to see
as grasshoppers nibble
my tomato plants.

          My mother screamed
at any spider, no matter how small; she shrieked
and flailed at it until someone came
and killed it for her.

I refuse to be my mother.
This is neither recluse nor a widow,
arachnids we humans are right
to fear. Aha! There she is, an orb-
weaving garden spider!

          I open the window,
slide a spatula under her, deposit her
in a pot of oregano on the deck,
smiling as I do this small service
for a world where so many people shudder
in the grip of despots.

Chapter Two: The Spider in the Bathroom Window

Two months ago, I slid a spatula
under, left her on the deck where
she could build a new web
in a world wider than a window.
Today she's back.

        Or else some newcomer
has decided the bathroom window is her home.
She clings quivering to the screen
as the wind blows, then leaps and takes
a fly for lunch. Another chapter opens.

Darning Socks

The minute my heel hits the hole in the sock
I feel the chill, and smile. I yank the sock off
grab the sewing basket, and rummage
for my grandmother's darning egg.
The smooth wood handle just fits my hand.
At once I see her face, glasses sliding down her nose
as she tips her head to focus on the needle.
Her hair was white and permed; I could not imagine
tilting my head to see the needle—as I do now.
This holey sock has brought her back to life.
When my mother finally ran from that vile man
who was my father—jumped on a train at midnight
with me in her arms—she fled to my grandmother.
Left me there while she got a job in town. Sometimes
she could visit on weekends, if she could find a friend
to drive her down those country roads. Grandmother
lived in an old house with a wood stove. Before sunrise
I'd hear the rattle as she shook the ashes down.
At breakfast, she'd pour milk into my tea,
remind me that we didn't tell my mother. "She'd say
it'll stunt your growth," Grandmother said, and laughed.
In the old log henhouse we'd gather eggs,
dump food scraps out as hens clucked around our feet.
Then we'd carry wood together, stack it in the wood box.
She held my hand when we went to the outhouse
on the gully's edge. Through my small seat
I could look straight down a rough cliff to rocks far below.
I'd read *Reader's Digest* to her while she crocheted.
"To save time, and let you practice your reading," she said.
She didn't like to be reminded she'd had to work while others
went to school. Today her smiling face watches from the wall
above my desk. I recall so much we did together.
But darning socks brings her back the quickest.

Anything that needs a stitch means
I can meet her in the sewing room.

On Her Deathbed

You'll find it all right there in my will. I've left
you fourteen boxes of books, a pretty varied lot,
from state history to mystery novels I've enjoyed.
In the basement you'll find six crates of family pictures.
I've labeled most of them but you'll have quite a job,
and you deserve it.

        Remember when you put
your report card under the papers to be recycled?
Took us quite a while to figure that one out.

        In the basement you'll also find
shelves full of Mason jars of produce I've canned from the garden,
everything we haven't used in years. I didn't label a single one.
You'll have to use your judgment to figure out
what's in each jar and if it's still good.

And you deserve it.

Remember the time you and your brother smeared
chocolate frosting over every cupboard in the kitchen?
On one shelf are a couple boxes of jewelry dating back to
my grandmother's time, and her letters I saved for sixty years.
Some of the jewelry is pretty valuable; you'll have to find an expert.
Each time I feel that dying and leaving you to sort all this out
is a terrible thing to do to you, I remember what
you were like as teenagers

        There just is no way to pay you back
for that night you and the Parker boy got halfway
across the state before your father caught you.

        But you deserve it.

What If

Just north of Chimney Rock I see the house, pink stucco,
and imagine settling down. A horse leans
against the plank fence beside the shed;
a pitchfork stands in a loose heap of hay.
On the sunset-facing porch firewood frames
a single chair. The chimney's stone: smooth rocks
gathered from that creek off west.

        What if I lived there? I'd saddle
up each morning, turn the mare upslope.
She'd pick a trail through lichened limestone boulders.
Sometimes we'd head for that blue butte
I barely see on the skyline. A two-track grassy trail winds
over and around the little swales toward pines and cedars
on that ridge. Is that a log roof? I know
just how the clouds sweep up behind the house.
Not much room for garden but it's sheltered by a cedar grove
beside the barn where deer find shelter from the snow.
The chairs inside those walls are made of pine, the table
where we'd eat beside the Warm Morning stove
would be worn smooth with scrubbing.

        Abruptly, I'm in Lusk.
If I lived here I'd walk to Decker's Market, chat about the weather
while the girl rang up my groceries. Eat at The Pizza Place,
maybe have a beer at the Silver Dollar before I headed home.
I'd walk the dog in the park, watch trains rumble past,
get a library card and choose books for an hour before a blizzard.
I like the two-story house standing tall beside Old Woman Creek's
dead cottonwoods; too much house for me, but I'd drop in for tea.
The neighbors who live there would notice if my sidewalk
wasn't shoveled, come check on me.

       Now I'm only thirty miles from home,
following a road I know. My grandma walked from her home in Edgemont
to the ranch in White Draw that her husband took to pay off debts
to his mechanic shop. Her son, my uncle, still lives there,
ninety-six last birthday and a little deaf, but just as determined
as she was to end his days where he was born.

There's another empty house, windows broken out.
The shed roof leans. I drive right past the cemetery
where my Grandmother Cora Belle still lies in gumbo.
"My stars!" she'd say if she could know I wrote
about her in a poem.

       That meager-looking place once belonged
to shirttail relatives of ours. I recall the cistern in the porch, the way
Aunt Rosie's arms bulged and flapped when she moved the concrete lid.
The dark pool underneath terrified me. A big steel sign displays
some stranger's name above the gate; did they fill in the cistern?
And that grave beside the highway, fenced, tree-shaded; a stone
with just a name and date tells all the story that I'll ever know.
Most who pass this way don't see it. I always nod respectfully, thank the one
who's buried there for this reminder of where we're headed.
Finally I top the hill and look; it's still there. The road I've followed
leads back to my own view, our dogs, my own man.

The Heron War

At dawn the heron stands like a thief in the reeds,
dark and silent as stone. I leave my bed
and sit in the garden to write what I see.
Near the ocean a thousand miles west,
flames ravage the forest like wars. Ash blown
over rivers and plains drifts around me like snow.
Below, on the pond, the heron spreads wings
like an angel of death. A raft of ducklings
tacks like a ship at sea, veering safely away. Sun
rises: a pearl in the smoky dark sky. Lady of Heaven,
we pray for a break in the heat, in the drought;

we pray for rain, for clouds tall and growling
with thunder and moisture. History defeats us;
autumn is usually dry, rain clouds absent until spring.
When this epoch's story is sung, hearts will break
at how little we knew of the future, of the fate
that was sailing that black ocean of hatred.

Linda M. Hasselstrom & James W. Parker

Things Worth Doing

There have never in history been so many opportunities to do so many things that aren't worth doing.

— William Gaddis, novelist; The Recognitions

Instead of talking on the cell phone,
watch the blackbird primp
for all the female blackbirds
heading north with spring.

Instead of jamming that earphone
into your auditory canal,
listen as the stars flap the stripes,
snow hisses over the lavender crocuses.

Don't read the editorial
about the council meeting, or

the column about exactly where
our strategy in Iraq went wrong.
Read a poem; read two!

Don't go to Disneyland in Orlando,
built over a former swamp.
Instead, find mud.
Lie on your belly beside it,
watch until something starts to grow.

Driving Across Coffee Flats

When I drive that ridge called Coffee Flats,
way out west of Edgemont, I look toward
Igloo, named because the Army
made the ground ripple with concrete
bubbles, sweeping white arcs that might
be ice, or snow, arches bowed and bent
like the curve of the earth itself. Instead,
behind steel doors, the Army once
stored bullets, powder, hand grenades
and bombs: neatly packaged Death
ready to be shipped out to soldiers
killing soldiers killing soldiers.
The earth does not forget.

Every time I drive by,
I expect to see black smoke,
hear the rumble of explosions.
The earth does not forget.
A lone ash tree
burns yellow among dun and ashen horseweed.
The road is a silver bullet looping
out of sight ahead, spinning and lethal.
Oncoming trucks' silhouettes loom black
as Panther tanks against the sun's
fierce glare. To my left roll blue hills
smooth as smoke, or perhaps a dream.
All promises hide in shadows
when I drive the ridge called Coffee Flats.

What thrives up here? Bull thistles and tall sage,
iron gates, barbed wire and distance.
Gray fence posts hold signs that read
"Private Do Not Enter." A dirt road twists
into the gumbo gully. Barbs of truth
snag the sad shine of plastic bags
from a city mall, limp and lying
about their wares to this arid, empty land.

When I drive that ridge called Coffee Flats,
I see an arch of rose quartz, sparkling still,
hand-laid with hope. Behind it stands a building
all gray boards and flapping tar-paper,
abandoned just below the cemetery.
Corrals are choked with
rough brown weeds.

When I drive across this ridge called Coffee Flats
I remember how the Texans trailed herds north
ahead of cowboys like Charles Franklin Coffee,
who liked the way the river curved
around the grass, came back to stay,
to build a family and an empire based on land
and money, became both a rancher and a banker,
he said, so he could hedge his bets.

The road drops down to cross a wash.
Yellow cottonwoods flare near those red rocks.
Green grass ripples like memory
along the river flowing slow forever,
passing Coffee Flats.

Was this the place?
Grandmother once told me of a rainstorm
that washed away the bridge while they shopped in town.
Her husband Walt eyed the gully, running with black water.
Shook his head. Got his axe out of the back of the Model T.
Felled two trees to span the flood. She tiptoed
across with the kids behind her, holding hands.
With his head out the window, he drove
the car out on that scaly pine bark bridge,
steered it safe across.

Linda M. Hasselstrom & James W. Parker

Seeing Is Believing

What I Loved in the City

Twelve years I've lived
exiled from the grasslands
where every sunrise
blasted gold into my eyes.
This October sun hides
behind a yellow screen
of cottonwood leaves,
lights the jumbled quilt
hung over the cracks in the wall.
My mother cut the pieces
when she was pregnant with her only child.
Me. Sixty years ago.
I pull the covers up
and decide to make a list.

Besides the man
I followed to this town,
what have I found
to cherish here?
What will I miss when we move
back to the ranch I love?

Trees: I'd never lived with them before.
When the furious winter wind wracks
the rattling windows, branches crack,
leaves twist off, spin into the street.
I turn the thermostat up
and still wear gloves in my office.
Thinking, I watch the spruce trees bow,
ladylike, their skirts a gentle shimmy.
I drive out of my way to float
down avenues where leaves blow
against the windshield. Walk the dogs
down alleys kicking leaves.

I discovered leaves in college.
I'd never lived with trees.
One fall night I left the college library
after midnight– (honest– the library!)
Walked across the campus ankle deep in leaves.
I was deep in some college girl's depression
until I caught myself kicking leaves,
laughing, kicking and giggling.
All the way back to that little dorm room.
After that it never failed:
I could cheer myself up
from nearly anything by kicking leaves.

I loved rain's clatter in the rusty metal gutters.
Hardly ever hear that on the plains.
Never hear the slap of tires on water
pouring down the street,
the single note of a robin closing out his day.
Loved the white dogs rolling in soft grass,
standing up to shake off dry leaves.
How street lights glow, haloed in fog yellow as cream.
The way an ordinary lamp shone
like candles in the dark behind drawn curtains
as I walked by outside. Cobalt blue bowls
on a yellow tablecloth I bought
for a dollar at the second-hand store.
The blooming branches of the crab apple,
the yellow currant. I cut them just for their scent,
placed in the center of that yellow tablecloth.
I'll take these with me to the prairie ranch
when I go.

Creed

I believe in eating beef raised on prairie grass, and killing my own meat.
I believe in rattlesnakes and coyotes, great horned owls and buzzards.
I believe in keeping my windows open until snow flies through them.
I believe the midnight breeze brings truth along with nightmares.
I believe in wool sweaters and socks, leather boots, and stocking caps.
I believe the joy of loving a dog is worth the pain of watching him die.
I believe in shopping in second hand stores, in "waste not, want not,"
I believe I should "use it up, wear it out, make it do, or do without."
I believe water can wash away most germs, but can't eradicate sin.
I believe those we love whisper in our ears after they are dead.
I believe in loose clothing and fences made of five tight wires.
I believe in skin without makeup, shiny with sweat or sun.
I believe in Henry David Thoreau, John McPhee and Mary Austin.
I believe in Nanci Griffith and Emily Dickinson and Mary Oliver.
I believe in green chile and in growing my own potatoes.
I believe in sourdough bread, in honey from a friend's hive.
I believe in horses, in Hereford cows and Black Angus bulls.
I believe in the purifying power of silence, and in poetry.
I believe in chickens chasing grasshoppers in the yard.
I believe in compost with potato peels and coffee grounds.
I believe in love. I believe in divorce. I believe in death.
I believe that what goes around comes around but
I believe we don't deserve everything we get, and
I believe we don't always get what we deserve.
I believe a hot bath will cure most of what ails me.
I believe in earth and buffalo grass and water.
I believe in wood and stone, and lightning.
I believe in loaded guns and sharp knives.
I believe in banjo music, fiddles and fire.
I believe in planting seeds in my own earth.
I believe in mittens and long underwear.
I believe in wind and in blizzards.
I believe we reap what we sow.
I believe in single malt scotch.
I believe, I believe, I believe,
and therefore I am

All I Know of Her

She stands on the board walk laid out
from the dark door. That low unpainted building
is the kitchen attached
to the two-story house beside it.
Rocks prop up one corner.
Behind her a single window is curtained in white.
Ahead of her, the walk ends in stepping-stones
that keep on going into the prairie.
She leans to the right on her crutch, but
no more than she must.
Her coat crumples
under her arm. Her wide hat perches
straight on her head, a handful
of straw flowers pinned in the center.
Her skirt hangs below her knees, her stockings
are black, her shoes sturdy and low-heeled.
The hat hides her face in deep shadow.

Is this the day she left her home to live
with her oldest daughter? Did she know,
when someone took this picture, that she
was never coming back?

She took over that homestead
after her husband died, raised their boys,
ran the ranch with their help. She married
again, birthed five more children, one of them
my father.
　　　　I brush my teeth while I squint
at the picture, three by five, framed in black
on my bathroom wall. I like to keep her close,
so I can look at her as I get ready for my day.
　　　　None
of her blood runs in my veins. But each morning
I start my day with her, wondering what she might
say if I could hear.

The Woman Traveling With Me Talks to Her Husband

Hi honey! How nice to hear from you.
We're fine; the roads are clear; not much traffic.
No, the bandages aren't in the storage room;
they're in the bathroom, in the medicine chest.
What did you do? Your jackknife? Do you think
you ought to have a tetanus shot?
OK, well, you take care now; call anytime.

Hello again—how's your cut? You found the Band-Aids?
Where's the hamburger? Look in the freezer. I'll wait.
OK, push that top basket to the left and look straight
down; got it? Good. What are you making?
Did you eat that roast I left for you? In the refrigerator.
On the second shelf. You could slice it cold
for sandwiches, or heat it with the potatoes and vegetables.
The potatoes and vegetables that are in the container
beside the roast. There's a sandwich mix too. It's in that
plastic container that says "Sandwich Mix."
There's macaroni and cheese in the refrigerator freezer.
All you have to do is thaw it out and heat it up.
In the microwave. OK, well, enjoy your sloppy joes.
Just look in the fridge; I left notes how to fix everything.

Hello again! The tomato soup? It's in my storage room
In the basement. On the second shelf there's a row
of all kinds of soup and there's plenty of tomato.
What's the matter? Oh, good, you had the pizza. No—you
mean you didn't eat it? I forgot to tell you to take the plastic
wrap off? It melted in the oven? That's why you made
sloppy joes. That cheese in the can? It's by your chair.
In the living room. In front of the TV. OK, talk to you later.

Grandmother's Hollyhocks

My grandmother lived
in an old bunkhouse, one room
with a screened porch where she slept
until snow drifted on her blankets.
The step was a block of sandstone
my Uncle George set solid at the door.

Outside, a dusty path in gumbo led
downhill to a low log chicken house,
corrals, a little barn with its back to the yard.
Behind the house, we walked through soapweed
and sage to the outhouse perched above the canyon.
From inside, I could look straight down the hole
to the crumbling edge of the cliff it clung to.
I tiptoed in, kept the door open, hoping to leap out
if it tilted over.

Finally, Uncle George put in a bathroom
just wide enough for a stool and sink,
with a closet in one end. She made do: kept
firewood stacked behind the big wood stove
hung curtains over cupboards made from
orange crates. To reach the highest shelf
she made a stool of tomato juice cans
sewn inside a circle of cloth.

Some Sundays, my dad
would say at breakfast, "Let's drive down to
your mother's." We'd finish the dishes, hop
in the car and go. We never called even after
she got a telephone, but when we drove
into that gray gumbo yard, she'd be standing
at her door, steam on her glasses, a chicken
frying in the big black pan.

"I had a feeling
you was coming," she'd say, pushing the glasses
up on her nose as she hugged me.

On the south side
of the house wild yellow roses twined
around a trellis. She carried rinse water
to them in her old tin dishpan. Nothing else
she ever planted would grow—until we took
a fistful of hollyhock seeds, scattered them against
the barn, along the side of the old garage. She'd tote
that heavy dishpan through the weeds, dribble water
along the dusty row.

Evenings she'd sit on the sandstone step
to brush gumbo dust from her stout black shoes.
Hollyhocks swayed, eight feet tall and spare,
rosettes of pink and yellow, white and red,
peach brilliant as her smiling face
against the gray old boards.

For years
I collected seed from her plants, from every hollyhock
I saw. Now they stand on all sides of my prairie house,
sturdy through drought, their leaves tattered
by gnawing grasshoppers. Two shades of pink,
blood red, pale and deep yellow, white and peach,
purple and even lavender.

Never black. These
stately hollyhocks cannot be picked. Not for them
the crystal bowl on the dining table, the tall
vase in the living room. They are independent
blooms that live their lives outside,
bear winter's cold and summer's blistering heat,
and thrive.

Like my grandmother, like all those pioneers
that came before us to this arid place,
they make do with what they have.
They don't complain or wither if the rains don't come.
They persist, endure, survive and persevere, prevail.

How to Make Rhubarb Sauce
— *for Hazel Hasselstrom Yuill*

Wearing a hat, tall boots and leather gloves,
head for the garden, protected
against sunburn, and rattlesnakes
that might nap or hunt among
the red stalks, cool beneath
the broad leaves. Sweep
the leaves aside; listen
for the rattle, watch
for the tawny body. Slide
your hand down the stalk. Grasp
it firmly and pull—never cut.

In the garden, cut the leaves
away, leaving them to enrich
the garden soil. Trudge home.
Fill the sink with cool water.
With a sharp knife cut out
bruises from hail, and dry spots.

Put the cutting board beside
the sink. Slice each stalk

into one-inch lengths; measure
out eight cups—two quarts—
chunks of rhubarb green and pink.
Place an inch of water in a large pot
with the rhubarb, one fourth cup
of sugar or honey. Or molasses dark
as a prairie night. Simmer gently until juice
begins to flow, then turn the heat
up a little. Stay in the kitchen. Boil
until the stalks begin to lose their shape.
Taste often. Add more honey or sugar,
orange rind if you have it.
When the sauce thickens,
cool and freeze.
                There.
You have made rhubarb sauce
for dessert, or to put on ice cream.
And your grandmother is smiling at you, remembering
rhubarb, and the farm where she once lived.

Linda M. Hasselstrom & James W. Parker

The Spell Checker Suggests

placenta instead of place mat,
but what I want to write about
is how the place mat in the café
beside the stock yards
is decorated with brands
used by the ranches
that surround and feed that town
perched on the parched prairie.

The place mat covers the scars
of brands carved into the tabletops
of this little stockyards café
by generations of cowboys
waiting for their cowgirls,
or the check for the sale.

Perhaps a placenta will
eventually appear in the poem
because placentas are central to calving
even if the cowgirls aren't pregnant.

But for now, all I want is a place mat.
Place mat I type firmly.
Placenta, says spell check.
Place mat. I hammer the keys.
Placement, says spell check.
Place mat I type, muttering.
Place mat.

Walmart Prayer

Our Walmart, which art everywhere,
Hallowed be thy name.
Thy truckloads come, thy will be done
in small towns as it is in metropolises.
Give us this day our daily lipstick,
and ignore our poor credit rating,
as we restoreth our credit with new debt.
Lead us into aisles of goods
and deliver us from the eyes of the floorwalkers.
Thy cheap cosmetics from somewhere shall protect me.
With Walmart as my guardian, I shall not want.
Walmart leadeth me beside the cases of veggies
from Mexico, and maketh me to lie down
on mattresses from China. Yea though I
walk through the parking lot surrounded
by muggers, I will fear no loss of credit.
Walmart seduceth me with glittering goods for which
I shall pay for the rest of my life,
and forever and ever shall I move ahead
waving my plastic credit card,
pushing the silver cart,
for Walmart is the kingdom,
and most of the power
and the glorious profit

forever and ever. Amen.

Sorting Hollyhock Seeds

Several friends have asked, so
I've filled a cookie sheet
with buttons of seed
from the yellow hollyhocks
that bend and sway in the garden.
The seed pods are furry, even prickly.
I rub my hands together, letting black seed
fall into the tray, tossing the fuzzy casings
into a bowl. I'll give the sorted seed
to friends, but I'll strew their shells,
those carapaces, along the outside of my house
because I know they've kept some seed hidden.
I'll kick a little dirt over the woolly pods as I walk,
and all winter know the promise of bloom
is tucked beneath the winter ice, ready
to sprout when spring softens snow to rain.

Choring Around

***When I'd visit my grandmother Cora Belle Hey and ask her what she'd been doing, she'd say,
"Oh, just choring around." She was doing all those little jobs women do to keep a household running.***

— *Another poem for Jerry Ellerman.*

What will I fix for lunch? Are
we out of potatoes? No, but
this one's spoiled; into the compost.
Here's some frozen round: I'll make Swiss steak.
Put oregano and basil on the list.
Canned tomatoes sizzle in oil.
I need to get to the accounts today.
Bank statement. Has the sun thawed
the dog waste so I can pick it up?
I can make the bed while the steak sears.
These are the sheets I bought from
the neighbor across the alley just
before we moved, my favorite shade of green.
Big envelope for the 1099s. Now get out
the pressure cooker for the round steak.
We could take the dogs for shots
when we go to the dentist—
no, we couldn't leave them in the car.
Make a separate appointment.

                              Headlines say
the Haiti quake killed 50,000 people.
That would be two-thirds of the town
where we shop. I remember that tiny tremor
we felt once here. Hard to imagine a real
quake. Snow is melting. Grouse graze
the brown grass outside the bathroom window.

50,000 people. Add garden seeds to the list.
Note to Trudy. What does she think
about this new abortion bill? Suzan will call
at one. I hope her daughter is doing better
in that new job. What is that dog doing?
Take out the compost. Put the recycling
in the garage. Did I put potatoes on the list?
I'd better do a full backup today. That stack's paid;
this stack's income. Where's my checkbook?
Stapler. Blast—my hair is too short to tuck
behind my ears. I never think to scrub the backside
of the faucet handle. That's a golden eagle
on the light pole. Ah--warm enough to air our
pillows on the deck chairs in the sun. Where
is that receipt? Oops—check the pressure
cooker. Just in time. Wonder how many
calories I burn running up and down these
stairs? 50,000 people. My wrists are sore from
kneading bread yesterday. Did I clean this
toilet today?

Jerry calls to ask if I want to go
to town for lunch. Asks what I've been doing.
"Oh, not much," I say. "Just choring around.
But lunch is nearly ready. Come on up anytime."
From her place above my desk, grandmother smiles.

Bottling August

— *for Cathy Beard*

Plum gumbo, plum gumbo
I hum as I wash plums in the sink,
slice oranges and lemons,
yummy plum gumbo
plums so taut with juice
the skins burst beneath my teeth.
August blooms in my mouth.
Bees buzz in memory.
Sultanas next, and walnuts,
I chop and simmer,
scenting the house.
                  Juice dripped
down the stems, down my arms
as I plucked each one from a branch,
pink deepening to red, to maroon.

Bees buzz against the screen
as the sweet juice simmers gently.
The jars stand gleaming and ready,
lids steam on a white dish towel.
First, I put a dollop on a white plate,
watch to see it thicken. Then pour.
A river of plums ripples
into the jars. I tighten the lids.
August is captured, cooling toward winter.

Some cold December day, I'll open a lid,
dip a spoonful of August to warm the morning.

I'm Writing Poetry in the Garden

But perhaps I use both those terms loosely.
Poetry is what I'm hoping to write
as I sit in this chair against the wall
looking at the space I call my garden:
two low raised beds we framed in discarded
warped railroad ties. We stacked and fastened them,
filled them with dirt dug from the creek bottom.
Each year I buy Early Girl tomatoes,
plant six or eight of them in cages that
protect them from the wind, and tuck some herbs
and flower seeds between the plants.
                              Against
the western concrete wall stand several pots
I've filled with dirt and more seeds that I've gleaned:
bachelor buttons, coneflower, Maltese cross,
evening primrose, gaillardia, and more.
They'll bloom all summer.
                              Last week I planted
radishes, oregano, columbine.
I cut the old vines off their trellis. Now

the light of afternoon shines on the threads
of silk spun out by spiders migrating.
The sorrel is three inches high. Rabbits
trimmed each leaf that wasn't inside my fence.
Outside the wire, I see one culprit now,
gobbling grasses among the windbreak trees.
The sun glows white through gray
                              and threatening clouds.
My man comes up the hill from his workshop,
collects our latest books, brings drinks for us.
Together, we read in separate chairs as
the red grass glows deep pink on distant hills.
Three tree swallows perform the dusk ballet
to songs of red-winged blackbirds, meadowlarks.
A robin zips into her hidden nest
in the rafters of the overhead deck.
A grackle squadron flies past in a vee.
Now there is poetry in our garden.

What Remains in the Barn?

After my dad and husband died, I leased the ranch
a neighbor runs his cattle in my pastures now
I still look out and see them grazing, wonder if
that cow off by herself is sick. I tell myself
they're not my cows, but some habits just don't die. I look
the other way and see corrals my father built
and kept in good repair. The neighbor used the chute
the other day to load a bull that broke a plank.
I haven't seen the neighbor since. The board just hung there
banging in the wind until I got a maul
and nails and boards and wire
                                        and fixed the damn thing right.
The neighbor never goes inside the barn. I've watched
the roof sag lower every day.
                        Today I throw
the big doors open. Time to take a look inside.
When we sold the draft horses, or they died,
we hung the harness in the loft. It's all still there:
blinders and breast collars, harness and nose bands, reins,
double trees, martingales, straps and snaffle bits, throatlatch
and curb chains.
The shelves hold brushes and curry combs, boots
and hoof picks. I find horn weights; once we raised
registered Hereford bulls.
In a manger I see a tangle of blankets, half a bottle
of whiskey left by the drunk we hired who lasted a week.
Stirrups and feed sacks hang on the wall.
A brown bottle gurgles:
medicine prescribed for some cow long dead.

We put the poke on cows that tried to climb a fence;
the spikes caught on the wire to keep them in. Old paper bags
of cattle cake.
            A long steel pole—the calf puller—
has a strap that fit around a cow's rear end,
chains we'd loop around the ankles of the calf
to pull it out. But when the cow began to fight,
she slammed us both against the walls. We pulled a calf's
feet off once; my father couldn't bear to kill it.
For days that calf stumped around the barn, trying
to walk on the ends of his ankle bones. But he nursed.
His will to live was strong. I don't remember if
he died or if my father couldn't stand the sight
and finally killed him
                        My dad's old coveralls still hang there on
a nail. He pulled them on when jobs got really messy.
My mother wouldn't wash them so he left them here.
That auger in the corner: once he grew some corn.
Hammers, chisels, branding irons, rosettes
from fancy bridles, ice tongs, halter for a calf,
stiff, unwieldy leather straps turned black with age.
What's the use of keeping it? The rancher who
leases this place calls the vet if he has trouble.
I back the pickup close, throw in the coveralls,
pause to cry remembering when he hung them there
the last time
                Two years ago I gave my saddles
to some neighbor kids but this feels more like death.

I Need a Walk

The words flowed through my brain
gurgling and splashing all morning.
Then stopped, like a faucet turned off.
So now it's time for a walk
Outside my door, flax stands
in blue pools, promising rain.
A red-winged blackbird zings around me
carrying a worm, dives into the cedar.
Hidden chicks cheep like water trickling.
The blackbird on the branch sings
like a waterfall. On the pond below
the house, a heron poses in ripples

From soil black as a well in the garden,
I pull spring onions, radishes.
Rhubarb leaves swoop like fountains.
And there: rabbit fur scattered across
the path. The coyote pups dined well last night.

Prairie Choir

Doves mourn from the trees around the old house.
Cows bawl for calves, sorting themselves toward night.
Crickets creak in the brome grass. One coyote
or twelve croon just past the horizon. Dusk
falls. Wild yellow roses perfume the breeze.
Nighthawks peent overhead, then roar, diving.
A killdeer bobs, runs, cries along the road.
Wind tinkles the hanging chime as dark creeps
like fog through the short grass. A bullfrog croons
from the pond. A baby rabbit nibbles
grass. Meadowlarks' chorus goes on as clouds
turn pink to the east. For ten miles that way,
a mile west, two miles south and a mile north,
I am the only person listening.

August Cloud

I move with dignified calm
out of the western hills.
Deep gray froths to white below,
in a heaven of eggshell blue.
Lightning flashes,
thunder roars and rumbles;
hailstones freeze and form,
armies of cold carry knives of ice
with cutthroat sharp edges.

Let my soft breezes ruffle leaves,
bachelor buttons and sweet peas;
asters and pinks waver and sway,
bullfrogs call from the pond.
My shadow looms, ascends,

covers the plains. Nighthawks dive.
Darkness covers houses
and towns, obliterates birds,
shrouds the sun. People scurry

to cover their garden stuff.
Silence drops. And then:
it begins with one *whock*
of hail on the roof. They wait,
heads tilted, begin to hope there will be
No more. Another. One more.
The bombardment begins, a cannonade
pulverizing their hopes and tomato plants,
peppers, and dreams of a harvest this year.

Seeing is Believing

Dusty green flows over pasture hills;
green gushes from the honeysuckle bush,
yellow blooms drift over buffalo grass.
I ride my rumbling four-wheeler along
the barbed fence, collect winter's shredded plastic,
crinkling its fake promises into my pocket.
Exhaust flavors my tongue. Snipe's shivery laugh
glides overhead, cascading on the wind
with the scents of sage and the bread
I baked this morning. I kneaded seed-filled dough

until it pushed back under my fingers
like a feather pillow. Waterfalls of bird song
flood over me; oceans of perfume pour
over the grass.
        Fog smudges it all.
Every sight blurs into mist behind
the cataracts growing on my eyes.
Across the hillside of my mind glide
seventy years of prairie views.

The End of a Beginning

Adaptation
— for Mary Ellerman

That black speck in the corner of my eye
is never going away. The doctor says this
is not unusual for my age.
                    "Get used to it," he adds.

Years ago, a surgeon wanted to operate on the knee
the horse stepped on. I wouldn't let him. Eventually
I traded my horses and my bicycle for a four-wheeler.
The knee collapses sometimes, but
                    I'm used to it.

Mary writes that she's learning to order
her groceries online. She'd rather drive to the store
but the traffic is too heavy. Now she doesn't
have to lug them from the store to the car,
from the car up the long stairs in to the kitchen.
The store delivers everything to the front porch.
"I like the convenience. I just have to
                    get used to It."

We discuss how aging affected our fathers, grandfathers.
how they ran into the side of the garage a few times before
they started parking outside. My dad pulled over on the highway
for "a little nap" to the dismay of Highway Patrol officers,
who admitted a roadside nap is not illegal.
My mother learned to take a nap herself.

> She got used to it.

One friend told me of seeing my parents parked beside
the highway, old gray heads lying on the seats.
Afraid they were dead, she drove on past.

After a while, the neighbors had all seen them
napping along the highway; they all

> got used to it.

I pick up a pen and begin proofreading this book
I started this poem when I was sixty-five. Now
I'm seventy-seven and have sixteen books
in print. The doctor's dead. My parents are dead.
The knee still bends. The black speck in my eye hovers
just below the lines on the page. I've

> gotten used to it.

The End of a Beginning
— For Jerry Ellerman

From my breakfast table I look east
above corrals and barn to where
buffalo grass rolls on without a break
until it meets the Badlands' colored clay.
For miles it spreads, a tawny green that's bare
except for barbed wire, coyotes, cows and grass.
And there it stands: a single house of stone.

All we know is in the county history:
Bill said he'd lived in Cleveland and Chicago.
In 1898 served in the Army
based in Florida; married once.
Drove jitney busses, worked on cars.
In 1912 he hired on with
Charley Upham on his ranch

He also filed a homestead claim—
six hundred forty acres in Urban township,
built his house of native stone
he picked from his own ground,
still mostly rocks today. And here's a picture:
Bill stands smiling on some urban street,
suspenders showing, hands on hips, looking
straight into the lens, an honest face
with not a thing to hide.
                    In 1917,
he made his ranch a full-time job, ran cows,
farmed some. He was a charter member
of the Urban Grange. When Bill got sick
in 1946 he moved into the Soldiers Home.
He sold his ranch to us, then died in 1950.
Military rites. They say he had
a step-child lived in California.
There the story ends, below Bill's smile.

Nineteen seventeen to forty-six:
almost thirty years he lived there in
that house of solid stone, the only place
for miles.
            All we can do now is speculate.
I recall peeking in the windows
when I rode that way to look for cows.
Father told me never to go inside.
I could see a hand-carved fireplace, shelves,
dishes in a cupboard and a stove.
                    One day in 1952,
I tied my horse, climbed through a window.
On the floor were tiny envelopes,
matching cards printed "William Snable."
I stole some, hid them for years. I wish
I had them now.
                    I remember one thing more: a small
notebook with Bill's records of all that
he bought for his "bungaloo." My dad's
step-brother Ed stole the book too,
took it with him to Camp Pike when he
was drafted. Nineteen and seventeen,
and Bill was still alive. The Army
sent it back with Ed's "effects"—
all I have left of either man today.
                    I know now that
when I trespassed, Bill had been dead two years.
Hailstorms had broken windows. The roof
began to leak. Birds nested in the second story
but the stones he set held firm. The house stands
there yet.
            From my breakfast table I
look east, and every day
I greet Bill Snable.
I think of how his stone house
has stood through all these years of blizzards,
drought and fire and rain. I wish he knew.
Perhaps he does.

Cooking Up Poetry in the Kitchen

I promised myself that after lunch
I'd go to my office to work on poems.
Instead, I'm washing dishes.
                              Why shouldn't I write
poetry in the kitchen? Like most women I spend
a lot of time here, making poetry to eat.
Right now there's granola in the oven
and two heads of lettuce in the sink.
I'm sipping a mocha made from my own mix
and what remained of coffee from this morning.
There's sun tea brewing on the deck
                              Of course
it's all decaffeinated these days. I recall
how strong the coffee was I used to drink
on the night side of the Sioux City Journal. Alex,
the Sports Editor, dumped whiskey in his last cup
when the presses started rumbling at midnight.
Ross would be dithering about an obit,
Lucas consulting his book on grammar.

Already, poetry in the kitchen has escorted me
back in time. I hadn't thought of that job
for years. Now I can see those men I worked with,
their tired smiles. Chuck, hands smeared with ink
from the press, brings in the front page.
I remember dawn's chill as I stumbled
down the street to my car when the night shift
was over. And now I realize they must all be dead.
I was the new reporter, fresh out of J School,
hired because the young men, drafted,
were being shot at in East Asia.
If I'd been writing
this poem in in my study would I have thought of them?

Granola's done. Thunder roars. Outside the wind
is beating on the stalks of a dozen hollyhocks
with yellow blooms. It's time to go downstairs
and see if I can find the poem I'd have written
if I'd gone down there an hour ago.

Do Little Things Count?

All day I nibble at little jobs: scoop
hair out of the shower drain, hang
fresh towels, throw away the twisted
toothpaste tube.
                    Today I cleared a shelf
above the sink, arranged
an orchestra of deep red and blue light:
bowls, glasses, a pitcher, a bottle, a slender vase,
a fluted glass with a clear stem.
Each day, washing dishes, rinsing,
placing them in the drainer, I will pause and look up,
smile as the sun makes radiance in the day.

The Bullfrog on the Pond

Spring's first sultry day slides gently toward the dark.
From her nest beneath the deck a robin glares
as I sit down. Her mate trills from the gate. The siding
ticks as day's heat seeps away. The pond is shrinking.
Water plants rise pink with bloom from muddy depths.
Ducks glide. *Baroom! Baroom! Baroom!* The bullfrog's call
resounds across the water, pulses through the dusk.

Inside a yellow columbine, a bee is humming.
The blooms have always made me think of tilted bonnets,
covering the ladies' faces in Victorian times:
silk for Sunday, purple plumes arising from
each bonnet's back. Each pod becomes a sheltered womb
for next year's blossoms. There it is again: *Barooom!*
The bullfrog lets us know that all is well.

The Evolution of Green Bean Preparation

When my grandmother snapped beans
she sat in sunlight on the block of sandstone
that formed the step to her small house.
She'd picked the whole beans
into the yellow crockery bowl, dropped
broken beans into the green one.

I stand at the sink under an electric light,
my back to the windows' glare,
snap the ends into the compost bucket.

She tossed the beans' ends into the yard.
Her chickens collected, tilting their heads, to peck.

I try not to hear the highway's
rumbling hum or listen for a hen's *cluuuuck*.

She admired blue peaks across the valley,
fat red cows grazing foothills.

I notice brown spots on my hands;
Toss broken beans into a plastic bowl.

Crocheting, she'd simmer the beans with
ham bones, scenting the house all afternoon.

I'll steam my beans with olive oil,
healthier than ham fat.

She relaxed into the coming dusk,
watched the sun slip away from the hills.

I wash my hands, hurry to my desk
where I start a poem before lunch.

On the shelf above the sink
Stand her green and yellow
crockery bowls, too fragile to use.

Undecided Poems

— *For Hobie and Lois Morris*

Today I'm sorting poems:
these are ready to submit
but those need work.
Sometimes I find the same poem
in two different files.
                    Ruthless
today, I choose, make corrections,
cut the duplicates into grocery lists.
Some, like leftover steak, seem too good
to throw away. I write letters on the back,
fold and tuck, and mail them off
to friends who read in winter
beside their wood-burning stove.
                    One day
soon these attempts at poetry will nest
among the ashes, flare and breathe
as they never did in my hands, lead
flame to ash or oak, living words
to keep my good friends warm.

Counting Dogs: A Poem Still Unfinished
—*For Jerry Ellerman*

Once I read an essay by a man who
calculated his age by dogs he'd had.
"I am six dogs old," he wrote. Six dogs old.

Today I will place another white stone
on the heap of quartz I have collected
on my daily walk, remembering. Schnitz
was round and short; his hair shone
black and brown. A ranch dog. He
tolerated me.
            When I moved to the ranch
I was nine years old. One day I was walking
to the outhouse on the old board walk when
he leaped ahead, killed the rattlesnake beside
the path. He led me safely through the fields,
chased cows away from gates, rode in
the pickup beside my dad. He had one
bad habit: he always chased the mower
when we were cutting alfalfa for hay.
One day the hired man came in sobbing, asked
for the rifle. "Cut his back legs off." I heard
the shot but never knew where Schnitz
was laid to rest; the hired man did that too.

Teddy was my mother's dog, but he loved
me without restraint. I brushed his soft curls
every single day, black and brown mingling,
ten years until I went off to college. Mother
told me he lay on my porch every single day
until he died, refusing to eat, waiting. I hope
I can apologize to him again someday.

My mother got a black dog with curly hair
she laughingly called by a name she knew
I would refuse to say. "His name is Blackie,"
I told visitors. Mother snickered.

I married, moved away, got the Scots Terrier
we called MacDuff. My husband took
him to a city after the divorce,
abandoned him with a discarded
girlfriend. I tracked him down,
dognapped him back to the ranch
just in time; he's buried on that knoll.

For a while, I kept cats. Then I met big George
who had little Loki the white poodle
until someone fed him poison.
We found Leif the Norwegian Elkhound
living under a rock in the pasture,
dining on dead calves. We took him camping;
he grew infamous for stealing steaks.
He'd come running back to camp
pursued by angry men. "Haven't seen him,"
we'd say, while he hid inside my sleeping bag.
While we were visiting a friend, he killed
a goat that turned out to be the mascot
of an Air Force base. The next day, he vanished.

Cuchulain the Westie hated men who wore hats
but accepted bribes of hot dogs.
One day we left him outside our house
while we went to town. When we dropped off
their groceries, my folks told us
"Your dog made a racket all day long."
He wasn't in our yard. We found him
in the open well pit beside their house.
Drowned. All day he'd paddled
and barked for help. We buried him on this hill
where he always waited for us, put up
one white stone for him.

Frodo was a Westie puppy who
grew so faithful to my husband
he nearly died when George did,
then kept me sane until he couldn't see.
Jerry held us both while Frodo went to sleep.

We gathered more white stones.

Duggan bounced the ragged purple ball
lived through the cancer operation,
never even whined; died on the couch
with Mac the rescued Westie close by him.

Rescued Toby had a broken leg. He made us
laugh the way he hopped around the yard
waving his pink and white cast.
He joined us at the ranch to keep Mac
company. Both of them walked with us
down to the barn every day,
white tails waving like plumes,
and helped me look beneath the hollyhocks
for mice and frogs.

At twelve dogs old, I said "No more."
But when Mac died, Toby was alone.
And then came the female we named Hattie.
They slept nose to tail and were content.
Ten. And now there's Hattie, all alone,
snoring on the couch. We buried Toby
yesterday. Eleven. Hattie can't hear me cry
and doesn't see too well. She misses Jerry,
follows my every single step.

                         You cannot count
those dogs you've loved, without remembering
all the good time that you spent together.
Begin. Count all those dogs that you once loved.
Recall their names, how cold their black noses
felt on your face at dawn, how their tails wagged
when you came home from school or work. Start now.

Postscript:

Hattie 1 died not long after I wrote the poem. Shortly afterward, a friend told me about another Westie who was about to be displaced by a baby in a family headed for Guam. "She stays in her crate," they told me firmly when I picked her up. Her name was similar, so I called her Hattie 2. When she wants to be alone, she goes to her crate in the closet. Otherwise, she sleeps beside my pillow. When I walk, she gambols beside me, wildly enjoying the freedom of the prairie. I'm thirteen dogs old. I've made sure Hattie 2 will have a loving home if I die first.

Cleaning the Greenhouse

— *For Jerry Ellerman*

You built me a beautiful tiny space
for growing things: recycled windows
surround earth contained by stout black timbers.
A workbench with shelves holds pots and tools.
The roof curves like a Chinese pagoda.
Along the clean white windowsills
I placed sand dollars I'd found walking beaches
far from this prairie grass. I started
with tiny ones, then a little larger,
looking at the leaf shapes on each one.
When I think of the greenhouse, I see it this way:
filled with light, with wheels of white sand dollars
spinning in the scent of green plants,
solidly rooted in rich earth.

This April day I face the truth:
dead flies lie in drifts along each shelf;
spiders crouch in corner webs.
The window glass is spotted,
shelves filled with plastic pots I'll never use.
Thinking of you, hoping you are headed home,
I clean each surface, wipe and polish,
dust and sweep, sort and toss.
The garbage can is full.
The greenhouse windows sparkle.
The sand dollars are still far from the ocean.
I tuck radish seeds into dark, damp earth.
A spider dangles in the rafters, ready to catch flies.
Satisfied, I sit on the old kitchen chair
saturated in sunshine,
Inhale the fragrance of spring,
and start a poem.

A Garden Poem

After spending all day at writing,
I am ready to relax--
but I need to water the garden.
So I sit in my canvas rocking chair
under the deck, iced mocha in one hand,
pen in the other, notebook in my lap.
Water gurgles gently at the base
of an Early Girl plant carrying twelve green fruits.
A weak tomato plant has fallen over.
I find a brace in the greenhouse, tuck it
gently into place. Sit back down. Sip mocha.

Coneflower blossoms twirl their yellow skirts.
Two bullfrogs sing bass from the muddy pond.
A wind chime jingles in a gentle breeze.
The anise sways. Bachelor buttons lean.
a butterfly lurches, clings, and sips
from a bloom. The centers of gaillardia
glow with volcanic fire beside the white
wimples of the Shasta daisies. The grape
vine is crawling up the concrete wall,
reaching for the greenhouse trellis. I grab
a paper bag and collect flax seed.

Vinca curls around a table leg.
Hummingbird moths sip nectar from
evening primrose blossoms. Which reminds
me to take down the hummingbird feeder
which has attracted only mold.
Time to move the hose. Grasshoppers are eating
the hollyhocks north of the house
but the green peppers thrive. My Valentine rose
is blooming for the third time. The dill
is heading out, vivid yellow. Only
a few berries cling to the currant bush.

Why did the radishes do so well in one place
and so poorly in the other? The clouds are drifting,

stretching frothy white against the blue.
A nighthawk calls over the pond, wings blurring
as it dives. Once more I've planned
to sit and relax, enjoy the garden.
Once more I've found a dozen chores to do.
My gardening: tending to these fertile beds,
the daily work with green they offer me,
the daily dose of poems?

Basil Harvest: A Recipe

Late August. Up at six, I'm picking basil while it's cool.
Traffic on the highway sizzles: bacon in a fry pan.
Cars speed along, unaware of the buck and doe
grazing in the field beside the road, ears swiveling.
Kneeling by the basil bed, I pull leaves roughly from
each stem. The licorice scent begins to warm my nostrils.
I leave the bucket in the kitchen, turn my mind
to poems in my office. This afternoon I'll wash
and sort the leaves, taste a few, spin them dry.
With my kitchen scissors I'll clip at random in the bowl

until the scent begins to overwhelm my senses.
I'll pack a single handful of the leaves as tight as possible
in a cup, then dump it in the chopper bowl.
I'll add a half cup of grated parmesan,
walnuts chopped, or almonds: a quarter cup.
A spill of salt, four garlic cloves. While the chopper
spins and slices, blending smoothly
all the flavors, I'll drizzle golden olive oil,
watch the way the colors shift, merge, fuse.

I'll taste and smile. Water boils for pasta,
supper for today, as well as for
those long tomorrows that will come
with snow and ice and blizzard winds.
I spoon the pesto into plastic bags,
flattened for the freezer. Deep in winter,
when snow the piles high against the windows, we
will taste the soul of summer's garden.

Once: A Love Poem

Love was once a long-stemmed rose with a price tag.
Now it is a handful of yellow roses from the pasture.
Love was once a bouquet of daisies at dinner.
Now I smile as I wipe your toothpaste from the sink.
Love was once sweet whispers in the night.
Now we smile, swap comics for the front page.

Love was once a dinner at the finest restaurant,
now it's the scrape of your shovel pushing snow off the deck;
once a filmy nightgown and candles at the bedside,
now your favorite roast and new potatoes in the oven;
once a shiny card with poetry inside,
now your hands in the dishwater after supper.

Love was once groaning and sweat-slicked flesh,
now it's the quiet of two crosswords after lunch.

Coronavirus Spring

Sunday:
Clouds coalesce under blue sky. Sun lies
hot on my face. Three redwing blackbirds sing
from three cedar trees, a liquid ripple:
a dozen tiny waterfalls chiming.

Monday:
Sorrel sprouts inch upward in sunshine; trucks
roar past on the highway, transporting all
we need to survive. Killdeer call, contend
over nesting space beside the stock dam.

Tuesday:
Cattle graze, moving slowly over grass
that's bronze and gold, with green just beginning
to show above the skin of the earth.
Trees grow, birds pull worms, wind blows.

Wednesday:
Overhead gray clouds rise into white fluff.
Higher, the sky is brilliantly blue
forever. Northeast, clouds are purple, black
and folding, piling up, bulging with rain.

Thursday:
The sweet high crane call draws our eyes upward
to long white fingers of cloud, blue-eyed
sky: there, circling, whirling, spinning north.
Yesterday they left the North Platte River.

Friday:
Beside the hillside cairn we built of stone—
granite, schist, rose quartz and white, gneiss, mica
feldspar—lie puffs of rabbit fur gray white
where coyote caught her prey and dined at dusk.

Saturday:
The cow that lost her calf last night lies still
beside him. She hasn't been to water.
The coyotes will be back,
but she will wait another day.
The redwing blackbird flips his tail and trills.

Sunday:
The earth is living normally for spring.
Going about the business of its life.
Only humans are confused and dithering.
Nature may never miss us, if we go.
Nature may be grateful, if we go.

After My Bath

Wearing only suds
I step out into cool night air,
into crickets and bird trills
dissolving into dusk, a big gray sky,
with corrugated clouds,
thunder a long way off. Here under the deck,
a dozen orb weavers strum octagonal webs,
waiting for inevitable mosquitoes. Gold light pales
on redgrass, vanishing from the green hill the way
tickling bubbles dissolve on my skin.

A redwing blackbird chirps. Something
rustles in a bush beside the wall.
The highway lies gray and quiet.
Beyond the fence, a calf bawls,
is answered by a mourning dove.
Time to go inside, lock doors,
look forward to another day.

Of Which I Die Possessed
— *With thanks to Chuck Riter*

Being of sound and disposing mind and memory
I hereby make and declare this to be my latest poem.
However, I hereby decline to revoke all former poems
which I have heretofore made. I direct my literary heirs
to make payment of all my unexpressed gratitude
to those who have caused my work to be published,
and to those who read it and smile or nod. I have left a signed
statement disposing of items of tangible personal property.
Intangible personal property is another matter entirely.

I hereby revoke all uncompleted outlines and scribbled codicils
that make no sense. Since I am unable to conscientiously revoke
all rough drafts, I request that unbranded synonyms, antonyms
and verse forms be set free to find new homes. Let my inspirational
bath tub be returned to the hillside to resume being a watering
trough for horses or free-roaming wildlife.

Being of sound and disposing
mind and memory, I direct that poems in the "nearly complete" file
be buried with me. As Joe Hill once said, "Who knows what may lie around
the next corner? There may be a window somewhere ahead. It may look out
on a field of sunflowers." Revision and resurrection may go hand in hand.
However, being of sound and disposing mind I also direct
that the rough drafts of poems that are clearly inferior
and the notes and residue which shall remain after collection
and publication of the good ones, be burned to ash
—carefully, in a monitored container so as not to set a prairie fire.
I hereby request and direct that the resulting ash be tossed
from the highest hill on my property—that one to the south—
be scattered over the garden where I grew tomatoes, and be flung
over the buffalo grass where I rode my horses.

If any legatee, devisee
or beneficiary, directly or indirectly, without probable cause, contests
or disputes the probate of this will, or maintains before any court or crowd
that this is not my last will, then I absolutely revoke any legacy, devise
or provision to such person. They get no signed books,

and certainly no rough drafts. I, Linda M. Hasselstrom, testatrix,
sign my name to this instrument on a day heretofore to be named,
and being first duly sworn, do hereby declare to any authority
that I execute this instrument willingly as my free and voluntary
act for the purposes herein expressed and that I am under no constraint
or undue influence.

On the matter of declaring myself to be of sound mind
I must defer to a greater authority since in some circles poets are automatically
and without recourse supposed to be incapable of being of said
sound mind. However, if anyone maintains before any court
that such power of poetry is not a valid power of poetry,
or contests or disputes any other poetry estate planning arrangement,
plan or scheme I have undertaken or implemented, whether *inter vivos* or testamentary,
or maintains before any court that such arrangement, plan, or scheme is invalid,
then I absolutely revoke the legacy, devise or provision to such person
and declare the same to be void and of no effect.

Making Do

— for Jerry Ellerman, with my love

After a hot bath in the tub you set in place,
and enclosed in polished wooden walls
and shelves, I dry myself and hang the towel
on a rack you made, slip on your warm socks,
the deep teal robe you bought me.
                                        I sit at the desk
you designed and built, with my computers, printers,
paper, notebooks, keyboards, ink and paper. Next
to me stand shelves with reference works, even
space for the turtles I collect to remind me to take
the time I need
                        That's all I have now. Time without you,
time in this home you created for us
                                        to remember all I've lost.

Lockdown

— *For Jerry Ellerman, again*

Dusk. Work done. You come to the house
from your shop, fix our drinks. I leave
my basement office. We sit in rocking chairs
under the deck. Sip and visit while the day's heat
subsides, the sun slides west
                           look up,
begin counting: twelve orb weavers rest
in deck shade on the edges of twelve
precisely-woven nets. A fly writhes
at the edge of a web. A spider
races out to wrap it tight in filament,
retires to the shadows.
                    Before us, in sunlight,
a grasshopper sparrow gulps to prove its name.
Two barbed legs scratch the air; the bird swallows
again. Early Girl tomatoes glow yellow and red
in sunlight. Marigolds jostle in crowds. Later we'll
play Boggle or Rummykub at the kitchen table.
We miss the meals and Bingo games at Senior Citizens,
but don't want to take the risk. No one wears masks.
For seven months now we've been wary, donning masks
before we shop for groceries, or fill the car with gas.
While many people fret, we are content to live
as ranchers used to do: once a month we go to town,
shopping lists in hand, an ice chest and recycling
in the back seat. We've mapped the city: bookstore, library,
hardware store. Groceries last. We don't stop for lunch
unless it's takeout. We've eaten in a park, but also in our car.
Before all this began, my Valentine gave me
a potted rose. Yesterday it bloomed again, blossoms
are pink and firm just like the first ones, back in winter.
Tonight we'll dine on homemade soup, ice cream
and blueberries for dessert, pronounce life good.

Walking: the Changes

The scrim of lacy ice beside the path
is fragile as the seashore foam
left behind the tide. The dogs
race across the layered snow without
regard for toenails skidding sharp
on freshly fallen frost. They slip
and tumble, right themselves and run again.
I pause to watch and then I step
off snow and onto grass at road-
side's edge. It's years since I began to see
old ladies taking smaller steps
on snowy days. But when did I
begin to think of falling more than of
the beauty of this brittle ice?
The grass is cushion to my feet,
bends to every step. My spine is rattling
in my body like a bag of dice.
I square my shoulders and look up
in time to see a shaft of light
shooting up from these bronze hills:
another day of life begins,
and once more I give thanks for sunrise gold.

Acknowledgments & Notes on Poems

Seeing is Believing, True Words, Story Circle Network;
pub. Vol 23 No. 1, March 2019

Bottling August, *Prairie Choir*, Tangled Serenity,
Scurfpea anthology 2021

Walking: The Changes Story Circle Network True Words
anthology 2020; Vol. 23 No. 1, March 2019; revised

The Spell Checker Suggests, Pasque Petals, Spring 2020

I'm Going to Have to Buy Another Ham, Oakwood, 2020

The title *The End of a Beginning* comes from a painting done
by artist Jon Crane of a rock house built in the early days by
Bill Snable. Jon Crane had spotted the rock house, located on
private ranch land in western South Dakota. We introduced him
to the landowner and arranged for him to paint the scene. At
Jon's invitation, Jerry titled the painting. He specifically said "A"
beginning rather than "the" beginning, thinking of the many
homesteaders who created lives in this area. Trespass is strictly
prohibited and dangerous; the rancher's cattle will not be
friendly, and the landowner definitely would not welcome you.

I started *Lockdown* 9/5/2020 but hadn't shown it to Jerry; he
was killed 9/18/2020

South Dakota Geographic Names, p. 512, says Coffee Flats lies
in Fall River County in a bend of the Cheyenne River, southwest
of Cascade Springs, and bears "a name of unknown origin."
However, Charles Franklin Coffee was a prominent rancher
in the area in the late 1870s. Born in Greenfield, Missouri in
1847, Coffee joined the Confederate Army at age 13, serving
in a regiment with his father for four years before relocating to
Texas. In 1871, he worked for the Snyder Brothers, driving cattle
north out of Texas. After one such cattle drive, he attended a
meeting in a livery stable in Cheyenne to discuss a vigilance
committee to deal with rustlers, possibly the beginning of
the Laramie County Stock Growers Association. He returned
to Texas in 1873, bought a herd of 1500 and, in partnership
with A. H. Webb, settled on Box Elder Creek, 65 miles north
of Cheyenne, WY. As the area was cleared of Indians and
made available to white settlers, he expanded into Nebraska,
eventually becoming a banker. In 1879, he married a distant
relative and childhood sweetheart, Virginia (Jenny) Ashland
Toney of Camden, AR. Settled in Cheyenne, the couple had four
children before moving in 1900 to Chadron, NE, when Charles
traded 2000 head of cattle for the Bartlett Richards home there.
He was active in ranching and banking until his death in 1935
at the age of 88.

Teton Science School (www.tetonscience.org) provides
wilderness experiences–such as identifying scat and building
a shelter of loose snow, called a quinzhe–for students pre-
kindergarten through grade 12. I presented a program there in
1988.

The Spider in the Bathroom Window was published online by
Prairieverse, with a Christian Begeman photo, on February 25,
2020, then revised after comments from a discerning friend.

Introduction to the Photographs

I grew up in western South Dakota, on a dude ranch in the Black Hills. When I was very young, my dad gave me a simple Brownie camera, a roll of film, and showed me how it worked. I'd wander around our property, aiming the little box at random subjects: my brother, our blind Cocker Spaniel Thumper, the dinner bell, horses. Dad would take the exposed film to the drugstore, and hand me a new roll to play with. I can't say that any of those early pictures were great masterpieces, but they did provide an education on seeing differently.

Later, my mom gave me her old camera, a classic folding model. It had adjustable shutter speeds, an aperture dial, and used medium format film. I shot quite a few images in junior high and high school, but unfortunately most of that film was stolen during a move in Chicago. As a high school senior, I was one of the few users of the photo lab nestled into a corner of the physics room. Mac Hymer, the affable old physics teacher, was kind enough to give me full access to the big Durst enlarger and the broad lab sinks. I learned to process my own film and how to make prints. Mac knew enough to let me be. My aunt sent me the first ten volumes of the Time-Life series on photography and let me use her 35mm Pentax. I was on my way to being a photographer even though I didn't know it yet.

I took a long hiatus from shooting after graduating college and entering the world of advertising. I learned how professionals approach their subjects. Working with many of the best commercial photographers of the day taught me how to visualize and execute my own ideas. I got my own SLR quite by accident, and traveled to Europe with it in the early '90's.

Fast forward to this century. A mutual friend introduced Linda and me, and I helped her publish *Write Now, Here's How*, and *When Hot Springs Was a Pup*. We got acquainted, first at the Hermosa coffee house, and then down at her ranch south of town.

When Linda brought up the idea of collaborating on *Walking: the Changes*, I felt it would be a great opportunity to pair some of my visual meanderings with her masterful poetry. She told me that I did not have to illustrate her words, but that I should feel free to do whatever seemed appropriate.

This book was a huge challenge. An enjoyable assignment. Creative people usually work best with fixed parameters and distinct boundaries, which this project did not have. Linda offered the creative freedom not only to provide the photographs, but to design and format the book.

Linda gave me the grand tour, showing me around Windbreak House, the barn, and the outbuildings. With permission to wander about, I tried to capture the essence of her grassland experience. I found inspiration in key phrases within the poems themselves. Some phrases suggested images that I had shot years ago. Some suggested places to visit with a fresh eye, like Coffee Flats, which I'd never heard of. Other images I've included here will challenge the viewer to discover a connection for themselves, if there even is a connection. My goal was to create visual threads and passages that weave between Linda's eloquent word pictures, to elaborate and enhance, to dance between the phrases visually.

A hearty thank-you to Ann Stanton, for bringing Linda and me together. And another sincere thank-you to Linda for providing creative inspiration and the opportunity to collaborate with one of South Dakota's most gifted voices.

— *James W. Parker November 2022*

Notes on Photographs

p. 6 - **Aermotor** – A lone water well stands idle on South Fairburn Road, near Hermosa SD.

p. 9 - **Bear Butte Barn Door** – There's a famous livestock barn southeast of Bear Butte, in Meade County. On this shoot, I walked around the structure looking for interesting details.

p. 10 - **Butte & Road Edgemont** – When Linda told me about Coffee Flats, some friends and I went exploring to see what remained. This lone butte stood out, in contrast to the miles of flat prairie near Edgemont.

p. 13 - **Stay Awhile** – This hotel is one of many semi-abandoned buildings in Fairburn, SD. I met the fellow who was renovating it one fall. He had hopes of opening it again as a bed and breakfast. He was gracious enough to give me a full tour of the interior. He'd replaced all the windows and done some structural work to insure the integrity of the building.

p. 14 - **Eastbound** – Fairburn Road, on a late fall day.

p. 16 - **Just a Buffalo Skull** – An artifact spotted along the Centennial Trail in Wind Cave National Park is a reminder of life and death on the prairie.

p. 17 - **Wings** - Linda found a dead blackbird on her gravel driveway and gave me these wings to photograph. The vibrant color against the Black Hills shale seemed a fitting tribute.

p. 19 - **Windbreak** – These cottonwood trees near the Rapid City airport seem to hold the clouds at bay on a hot summer day.

pp. 20–21 - **Fall into Winter** – Changing aspens near the dam at Sylvan Lake catch the late afternoon light. Sylvan Lake, in Custer State Park, is one of my favorite places in the world. The juxtaposition of the cool ice on the boulder with the alpenglow on the rocks caught my eye as I looked for different subjects this October day.

pp. 22–23 - **Out Near Wasta** – I've made many photographs near Wasta, on the Cheyenne River. Driving north out of the little town yields unique views of prairie, deep draws, and the occasional stock dam. Water is a key resource here in the West, and we build traps for it, catch it, and water the livestock with it.

p. 24 - **In Death** – Not a wolf, but a coyote, shot near the Folsom Church, along Spring Creek Road. The church has fallen into disrepair and displays graffiti on interior walls from vandals who have broken in to cause mischief. This poor creature was one of several deceased animals I ran across in the spring. I suspect it was caught raiding on a nearby ranch and caught a bullet. Interesting to note that I never see a coyote roaming our fields in Palmer Gulch, but I hear their mournful howling late in the evening and early in the morning.

p. 26–27 - **Wind Chill** – Owanka, South Dakota. Another railroad town on the banks of the Cheyenne, Owanka is largely deserted now. A majestic grain elevator, several abandoned vehicles, and some hard-working ranchers are all that's left of this once-prosperous community. The elevator is a popular subject among out-of-town visitors, and one that I have visited often. Owanka sees fewer tourists in the winter, however, which lends a certain appeal to this shot.

p. 29 - **A Bend in the River** – The Belle Fourche River, well north of New Underwood, is a tributary of the Cheyenne. The subtle color palette and the stillness of the water captivated me for some time. Shooting from the safety of a bridge on New Underwood Road, the view both east and west was quiet and peaceful.

p. 30 - **Chute Framed Barn** – Linda invited me out to her ranch as we embarked on this collaboration. I wanted to make some more personal pictures that dovetailed with my current body of work, "Stories Told in Things Left Behind", as well as telling her story. The cattle chute frames the barn perfectly.

pp. 32–33 - **Quiet Streets** – Merriman, Nebraska. The Sand Hills of Nebraska string together small farming towns like this one, with Main Street barely hanging on.

p. 34 - **Rollercoaster** – Another photograph of South Fairburn Road. East of the Black Hills, the prairie stretches endlessly, with gravel roads connecting the small towns and ranches.

pp. 36–37 - **Mormon Row** – The well-known barns and houses of Mormon Row, off Antelope Flats Road below the Grand Tetons. This is the John Moulton barn, arguably the most-photographed barn in America.

p. 38 - **Barn Door Vertical** – The door into the hayloft of Linda's barn appears to lead to a long step down but provides useful access for storage of hay in wintertime. Ranchers were often creative in using what they had to provide functionality.

p. 39 - **Cobb School** – Linda's Aunt, Anne Laura Meiners, taught school in this one-room school. The building was originally on Cobb Road, and was later moved to Highway 36 before being relocated again to Hermosa. Florence Cobb, Mrs. Lester Tubbs (Anna), Mrs. Lyle Hartshorn (Lena) also taught here, along with Mrs. Richard Meiners (Anne).

p. 40 - **Socks in the Drawer** – When Linda showed me around her house, I was especially intrigued by the colorful patterns of socks in her dresser.

p. 41 - **Leader of the Pack** – The concrete and steel dinosaur along Highway 79 leading south to Scenic, South Dakota has a long history. It was originally built by a shopkeeper to attract customers to his general store in Creston, along the highway. When the highway was improved and moved years ago, the town all but disappeared. But the green dinosaur remained and became a target for passing teenagers and vandals. In the late '90's, a group of students from the South Dakota School of Mines repaired the statue, giving it bike reflectors for eyes and mouth, and patching the holes in its side. My father told me about it, and he, my mother and I drove down to photograph it on a prior expedition. We were making pictures from the side of the road when my mother began jumping up and down.

"What's wrong, Ma?" I asked, as she shook her pants legs vigorously. In reply, a stream of red ants headed down her legs. She had been standing on an anthill!

This shot was made a few years later, after a successful foray down to Scenic. A passing hailstorm left beautiful light in its wake, and the horses pastured in the meadow added an amusing layer to the incongruous juxtaposition of dinosau.r and field.

pp. 42–43 - **Mountains of the Moon** – Badlands National Park, South Dakota. One of my favorite locations in the park; I was able to photograph moonrise just as the sun set, casting beautiful golden light on the jagged peaks of Norbeck Pass.

p. 45 - **Fence and Hills** – Elegant in its simplicity, this portrait of the prairie northeast of Rapid City was shot in fall, when the grass reflects the golden light of early morning.

p. 46 - **Tumble Inn** – A deserted roadhouse on US 26, west of Casper, Wyoming. In the summer of 2022, my brother and I drove out to Jackson, WY from the Black Hills. I couldn't pass this picturesque old restaurant without taking a photograph.

p. 48 - **Coffee Flats Schoolhouse Interior** – There are two separate Coffee Flats in the southern Black Hills. After trekking out past Edgemont and driving down Coffee Flats Road until it crossed into private property, I discovered this location on the map and made a second journey to photograph the historic school.

pp. 50–51 - **Out for a Walk** – Prairie Homestead, near Wall, South Dakota. It took many exposures to successfully portray this union suit hanging on the line at the historic homestead site.

pp. 52–53 - **Old Homestead** – I had permission to photograph on this ranch property south of Hot Springs on a search for windmills, horses, and old ranch buildings. I spent a good deal of time hiking around the fence line shooting the windmill, but came away with this shot, and another featuring the house and several horses that were my favorites.

pp. 54–55 - **Coffee Flats Road, Looking South** – Near Edgemont, Coffee Flats Road runs south, then west, then south again, with magnificent views across the verdant prairie.

p. 57 - **Coffee Flats Schoolhouse** – This school stands at the junction of Rocky Ford Road and Highland Road, near the Wild Horse Preserve south of Cascade. Used until the 1960's, the building was renovated in 2008. I heard rumors that this building was used in the filming of "Hidalgo", a movie starring Viggo Mortenson, but couldn't find any evidence to back that up.

p. 58 - **Drive Slowly** – The cattle guard leading to Windbreak House, Hermosa SD.

p. 60 - **Fairburn Fall** – South Fairburn Road leads out of town and up onto the prairie south of Linda's ranch. The cottonwoods in fall provide good color.

p. 62 - **Barn Side Door Wheels & Jugs** – Linda's barn provided some interesting details left near the workbench.

p. 63 - **Ida** – Ida Hasselstrom, as described in the poem.

p. 64 - **Bliss** – An autumn drive up north in Michigan leads down to the town of Bliss.

p. 67 - **The Right Words** – A studio still life, photographed to commemorate Dad's old Royal typewriter, which bit the dust years ago. TThe converted kerosene lamp came from Palmer Gulch Lodge.

pp. 68–69 - **Hollyhocks** – From Linda's garden.

p. 71 - **Garden Treasure** – Front porch on the old Duncan Manor in Towanda, IL, on Route 66. This large edifice has been bought and sold several times in hopes of renovating it for various uses. It currently belongs to a non-profit organization. More info: https://www.duncanmanorhouse.com/

p. 72 - **Chair In the Back** – A garden spot, peaceful and quiet, on the ranch.

p. 74 - **Barn Side Door** – Another view of Linda's barn, on the ranch near Hermosa.

pp. 76–77 - **Linda and Cows** – Hermosa, SD. Linda, Linda's current Westie Hattie, and cows in the holding pasture down by the Windbreak House.

pp. 78–79 - **August Clouds** – I am fascinated by clouds in their infinite variety. Storm clouds build over the plains in late August in the afternoon, often leading to hailstorms and a rainbow when the fury of the shower is over.

p. 80 - **Formal Portrait** – north of Wasta, South Dakota, on Elm Creek Road, this stately house is firmly posted "No Trespassing". While I was pulled off on the shoulder to make this image, a woman passed in her minivan, asked if I needed any help. Prairie kindness.

pp. 82–83 - **Open Range** – This iconic relic graces a pasture near Newcastle, Wyoming. Catch it on the north side of US 16, east of Newcastle a few miles.

p. 84 - **Windmill Blades** – Remnants of the Aermotor water pump leans against a shed on Linda's ranch.

p. 87 - **Kitchen Shelf** – Little things do count. This small collection of glassware graces Linda's kitchen.

pp. 88–89 - **Cirrus Over the Pond** – The hill above the stock pond, looking south from the ranch.

pp. 90-91 - **Moonset, Clouds, Range** – New Moon near Douglas, AZ, with the Chiricahua Mountains as backdrop.

p. 93 - **Hattie 2** – Linda's energetic little Westie investigates her home grassland.

p. 94 - **Greenhouse with Insulators** – The greenhouse that Jerry built, with some of the collection displayed on a handmade rock retaining wall.

pp. 96–97 - **Five Strands of Wire** – Another view of Linda's stock pond, with well-maintained barbed wire.

p. 99 - **Bath Water** – Fairburn Hotel, Fairburn, South Dakota. Relics awaiting reinstatement during the hotel renovation, neither with a fresh coat of paint.

p. 101 - **Windbreak House Chairs** – One of my favorite subjects are a pair of chairs, or a single chair in a unique situation. A moment of solitude awaits.

p. 102 - **Jerry's Quilt Rack** – One of the many handmade pieces Jerry built in the workshop.

p. 103 - **Gateway to the Sky** – Access to a pasture off Highway 79, south of Hermosa, South Dakota.

pp. 104–105 - **Don't Fence Me In** – The Oglala National Grassland, just south of Ardmore, South Dakota.

p. 107 - **Time Like a River** – Winter ice patterns in the borrow ditch near our ranch in Palmer Gulch. Often, small details like a blade of brome grass or a pattern in frozen puddles will provide an entire landscape in a small area. It takes practice to see these little landscapes, but once your eye is tuned to it, you will see them all the time.

p. 108 - **In the Spotlight** – A lone chair highlighted by the clerestory over the stage in the Fraternal Hall, Elkhorn, Montana. Elkhorn has been gentrified over the years, with just two buildings now preserved as a state park. Many of the private homes have been renovated as summer residences. When I was there last, the gold mine was once again being worked to extract what remaining minerals might remain.

p. 113 - **Tisdale Ranch** – This ranch house sits far out on the prairie between Wasta and New Underwood. The house has collapsed to the point where the north side is two feet lower than the south side.

p.115 - **Cottonwood Elevator** – One of the many abandoned grain elevators dotting West River South Dakota.

Front Cover - **Grass** – A single stalk of brome grass. I'm the first to admit that I know very little about prairie grass. We have brome on our land in Palmer Gulch, along with some alfalfa and timothy, and Johnson grass, but I'd be hard-pressed to tell you much more about these essential feed crops. We no longer farm our own fields, but have a local rancher cut and bale the hay in the summer.

Meet the Authors

photo: HJ Schmidt

Linda M. Hasselstrom

Linda started writing when she moved with her mother to a cattle ranch in South Dakota because she was going to get—as she told her teacher—"A horse and a father." She was nine years old, and her education in writing, ranching, and living began when her new father made her save her allowance to buy the horse. She earned the allowance by taking care of the family chickens, and herding cattle. After college and a variety of teaching jobs at colleges in the center of the nation, she returned to the family ranch. Her first published book, *Windbreak: A Woman Rancher on the Northern Plains,* was a diary of a year of her life on that ranch.

Her education in writing was conducted in the same way: by doing the work. Besides working as a journalist for several daily newspapers, she has constantly written and submitted her poetry and nonfiction. With seventeen books in print, she is now one of the Great Plains' best-known authors. She has spoken about writing and related topics for dozens of organizations and conducted numerous writing workshops for groups ranging in age from first grade to senior citizens.

https://www.windbreakhouse.com/

James W. Parker

The eldest son of South Dakota historian Dr. Watson Parker, photographer James Parker has always been fascinated by the architectural detritus and geologic history of the West. As an artist, he's interested in the effects of the passage of time on a human scale. His recent work *Stories Told in Things Left Behind* focuses on interior spaces and rural landscapes.

Quirky juxtapositions & peaceful grasslands highlight Parker's images. Whether photographing patterns of wind and water in a desert canyon, or focusing on the textures of a faded ranch, his visual commentary echoes the politics, history and cultures that collided in America's Westward expansion.

Parker also shoots on location and in the studio for commercial clients. Using a collection of strobe and tungsten lighting, his 30 years of agency experience and art director's eye bring a little extra to every assignment. Lately, he's brought his design skills back to the publishing world, founding Palmer Creek Publishing in 2020.

He's been known to photograph the occasional wedding and commercial assignments, although he's more comfortable with inanimate objects and large rocks.

https://www.parkerparker.net

Made in the USA
Monee, IL
29 March 2023

Walking: the Changes

Linda M. Hasselstrom and James W. Parker, both South Dakotans, find stories everywhere in the prairies and hills. His photographs tell stories of forgotten places and lives through light, shadow, and color, creating love stories to the land.

Linda's poems explore the same landscapes, finding humanity in the lands and people she knows and imagines. She can see herself walking to Decker's Market in Lusk, Wyoming, and she recognizes that corporate-created pollution in Bhopal leads husbands to divorce wives whose babies die in their wombs, but she saves a spider instead of killing it. She watches spruce trees bow like ladies, and tastes summer in the juice of a plum. Like all writers, she battles with autocorrect on her computer.

Here are two poets: one with words, one with photographs, collaborating to show their love and understanding of western South Dakota, creating a book filled with compassion, humility, and gentle humor.

--*Ann Haber Stanton,*
  author of "Deadwood's Jewish Pioneers"

ISBN 978-0-917624-08

POETRY
PHOTOGRAPHY
$29.95

9 780917 624087

LAME JOHNNY PRESS

PICTURE BOOK APOLOGETICS

PITFALLS

A Quick Guide
to Identifying
Logical Fallacies
FOR FAMILIES

BY J.D. CAMORLINGA